Meet Me at the Theresa

HOTEL THERESA
COFFEE SHOP · RESTAURANT
HOTEL THERESA
SKYLINE BALLROOM

Meet Me at the

THE STORY OF HARLEM'S MOST FAMOUS HOTEL

Sondra Kathryn Wilson

ATRIA BOOKS

NEW YORK • LONDON • TORONTO • SYDNEY

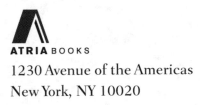

ATRIA BOOKS

1230 Avenue of the Americas
New York, NY 10020

ISBN: 978-1-4516-4616-0

First Atria Books hardcover edition February 2004

10 9 8 7 6 5 4 3 2 1

ATRIA BOOKS is a trademark of Simon & Schuster, Inc.

Photo on page iv by Cecil Layne. Courtesy of Terry Layne.

For information regarding special discounts for bulk purchases,
please contact Simon & Schuster Special Sales at
1-800-456-6798 or business@simonandschuster.com

Manufactured in the United States of America

To the memory of (Ollie) Jewel Sims Okala

Acknowledgments

In researching and writing this book, I was privileged to meet count-less people, mainly in Harlem, New York. These remarkable African-Americans inspired me, especially in view of the obstacles they endured during a number of the most turbulent times in American civil rights history. I would like to acknowledge them with my love and sincere gratitude for sharing their memories for this endeavor. Without their help, this work would have been drawn out even more.

My debt to the late (Ollie) Jewel Sims Okala, to whom I've dedicated this work, is enormous. She died during the early stages of this work. It was she who sustained my enthusiasm by constantly sharing with me her excitement for the story of the Hotel Theresa. Moreover, I owe her an incalculable debt for her devotion and commitment to my spiritual and intellectual development. She read the first essay that I published and every publication that followed until her death in 2001. She was a wonderful source of criticism, strength, and clearheaded common sense. The love and nurturing she provided sustained me throughout this process.

My agent, Manie Barron, of the William Morris Agency, offered practical, constructive suggestions that were helpful in countless ways. His devotion to the book and to my well-being gave me inspiration at critical times.

My editor, Malaika Adero, and editorial assistant, LaMarr Bruce, of Atria Books, offered useful suggestions that gave strength to the work. Their patience, thoughtfulness, and generous spirit will not be forgotten.

I am especially indebted to Wendalyn Nichols for her friendship and for helping me make sense of the research so that I could succeed in translating it into a coherent narrative.

Evelyn Barnes Parker provided constructive ideas and invaluable research assistance. I am grateful for her unselfish support and compassion displayed throughout. Her advice over the years has been priceless.

There are those who must be recognized for deeds that exceeded the expectations of professional kindness. Among them are Charles L. Blockson Jr., James and Jean Williams Booker, Gayle and Jim Carter, Evelyn Cunningham, Earl Davis, Ophelia DeVore, David Goldman, Ruth Guzzman, Danny Moore, Dianne Patrick, Mildred Bond Roxborough, Bobby Short, Percy E. Sutton, Jane White Viazzi, and Preston Wilcox.

I would like to include a word of appreciation to Henry Louis Gates Jr. and the late Nathan Irvin Huggins of Harvard University for the inspiration and support they have provided over the years. I have learned so much from them.

I have been blessed with wonderful friends. Their love and support have been invaluable to me both personally and professionally throughout the years: J. Yvonne Brown, Hazel Ferebee, Mildred J. Hudson, Paula J. Owens, Catherine Peppers, Raymond St. John, and Honor Spingarn Tranum.

I'd like to thank my family for their love, patience, and encouragement, especially my mother, Laura Clemmons Wilson, and my late father, William E. Wilson, whose love for history inspired me early on. I thank them for their encouragement and unwavering commitment over the years. Above all, I am grateful for their inspiring lessons about life. My brother, Michael Wilson, and his wife, Janet, never failed in their support and devotion. I wish to thank my sister, Patricia Wilson Pleasant, and her late husband, Joseph E. G. Pleasant, for their kindness and enthusiasm. Other family members who have been ardent supporters: Minta C. Brown, Sherwin Keith Bryant, Carolyn Craig, Wendi C. Jackson, Rufus and Jill Rosenberg Jones, Victoria Redus, Joyce and Benjamin Spaulding, Sylvia Thurman Williams, and Charles and Stephanie Wright.

I am especially indebted to Ella L. Spaulding who knew a number of the greats in this story. I am grateful for her love and support over the years.

Finally, to Michael, Jennifer, and Daria Stansfield, you have your hands around my heart. Thank you for enduring the graveyard shift. I felt your love circling me throughout.

Contents

Meet Me at the Theresa

Preface

The royal blue canopy over the sidewalk emblazoned with "Hotel Theresa" is gone. So are the handsome uniformed doormen who tried to quiet the chaos of the crowds clamoring to enter the hotel. Gone the policemen who ticketed the carelessly parked colorful Cadillacs that lined Seventh Avenue causing traffic congestion throughout the night. Gone the crowds of gawkers jostling for a place to peep through the venetian blinds into the Theresa's lobby where Cab Calloway, Lena Horne, Billie Holiday, Nat King Cole, Billy Eckstine, and Illinois Jacquet mingled and chatted.

The fifty-one-foot, J-shaped bar and its red leather booths that were jammed to capacity with good-looking and well-dressed black people have long since been sold for scrap. There are no more reefer-puffing jitterbugs or hepcats strutting around the hotel profiling and styling for the women they picked up. The ladies of the evening dressed in veiled hats, seamed silk stockings, and minks are no longer anxiously waiting to service men like Joe Louis and notorious gangsters like Bumpy (Ellsworth Raymond) Johnson, Red Dillion, and the Ross brothers. The Harlem street orators who stood outside the hotel on stepladders decrying the evils of white America have taken their preachments elsewhere.

You won't find many people who remember the Skyline Ballroom with its crystal chandeliers, high ceilings, mirrored walls, and velvet drapes, where ceremonious waiters scurried about fussing over placards and silver chafing dishes filled with decorative hors d'oeuvres for Harlem's upper class. And fewer still remember Bill Brown, the lothario who once presided over the hotel, whose mere presence would make women check their lipstick and men check their weapons.

Few people in Harlem know that the slim, white, thirteen-story building that stands on the historic corner of Seventh Avenue and 125th Street was, in its day, as famous as the Apollo Theater or the Savoy Ballroom, and more central to the history of Harlem than any other building there. For nearly thirty years, life in and outside the hotel was an exhilarating social experience that has not been duplicated since.

The year 1940 saw the coronation of the Hotel Theresa as the queen of Harlem. But for her first twenty-eight years, she was an unremarkable lady-in-waiting—a member of the minor nobility of Manhattan hotels, born of white speculators who watched in dismay as their exclusive white enclave was inexorably transformed into the undisputed capital of black America.

The Theresa Hotel made her grand entrance in the midst of a Harlem that had become the greatest village populated by the descendants of age-old Africa. Harlem was the black Mecca with a legacy so rich in dance, song, and literature that it was unrivaled by any other place in the world. Indeed, the black literary movement of the 1920s and the jazz explosion of that era had made Harlem an international phenomenon—a place "fabled in story and song," as James Weldon Johnson once put it.

Presiding over the most happening corner in America, the Theresa reveled in such triumphant times as Joe Louis fights, the *Brown* decision, two American wars, countless star-studded galas, and the birth of music genres like bebop and rhythm and blues. For most of its years as black America's reigning queen, it symbolized the epitome of what an oppressed people could do if given the opportunity to shine. The Theresa represented fame, success, erudition, and urbanity. It was the place where virtually every black person in America wanted to be, although most never saw it.

The Theresa was the axis for the hippest nightlife in the world when the hottest place to be seen was in the Theresa's bar. A walk in the neighborhood was not just a walk, it was strolling for happenings. There were the famous jam sessions at Minton's Playhouse, where bebop was born, the floor shows at the Baby Grand, the bevy of chorus girls who strutted their stuff at the Club Baron, the jitterbugs jumping all night at the Savoy, and the Apollo Theater and its string of showbiz heavyweights whose names graced its glittering marquee.

But the 1960s was the Hotel Theresa's last decade, and Fidel Castro's notorious 1960 visit turned out to be her final moment in the limelight. Looking battered and decrepit like a used-up prostitute, she had aged without grace and dignity. Once endowed with a rare elegance and grandeur, she became a has-been, a dingy flop. By the late 1960s when her doors closed, musicians, actors, pimps, and gangsters with policemen in their pockets had reduced her to the status of a common cathouse.

This story is based on unique, firsthand accounts. It's the biography of the hotel that has nothing less than Harlem itself as its backdrop, from the first influx of black residents, through the turbulent years when whites came uptown to cavort where blacks were not allowed, through cultural renaissance, social upheaval, and ultimate decline. It is a social history of the place that, more than any other in Harlem, was the epitome of a zeitgeist—and it is a collection of cracking good stories about and from the regulars, the celebrities, the owners, the workers, the neighbors, and the larger neighborhood. It tells of the gangsters and educators, the showgirls and the politicians, the entertainers and the wannabes, the intellectuals and the fast crowd who frequented the hotel, showing how the fates of the Hotel Theresa and Harlem were inextricably linked.

Come sit on the stoop with those who remember and watch the pageant of the Hotel Theresa—the iconic place that was once an elegant temple filled with the riches of the black world. Their stories evoke the spirit and grandeur of a hotel that was central to African-American life in a bygone era. They offer a unique opportunity to experience the sheer energy of a fascinating place that was the site and symbol of a people's multilayered culture. For everything that was important to Harlemites in particular, and to African-Americans in general, happened at the Hotel Theresa. The hotel has already achieved mythic status for those in the know; now *Meet Me at the Theresa* draws its history, more amazing than fiction, from those who lived it, so that readers can say, "I feel as though I were there."

I asked a former showgirl what the Hotel Theresa meant to her. She was thoughtful before answering, "It was a place where we had a good time. We had fun. If it didn't mean anything, you wouldn't be writing about it. We will never forget the Theresa. Never!"

One

THE NEIGHBORHOOD

The Hotel Theresa was located on the southwest corner of Seventh Avenue and 125th Street. Called the Great Black Way, Seventh Avenue has always been Harlem's most beautiful boulevard. This two-way artery, sectioned for uptown and downtown traffic, was divided by a narrow strip of beautiful trees and manicured grass and gardens. It was Harlem's principal business boulevard. Seventh Avenue mirrored Harlem's life. It had a number of beautiful brownstones, theaters, and apartment buildings that made it the grandest avenue uptown. The writer Wallace Thurman called the avenue Harlem's most representative boulevard, "a grand thoroughfare into which every element of Harlem's population ventures either for reasons of pleasure or of business. It reflects both the sordid chaos and the rhythmic splendor of Harlem." Pastored by Frederick Cullen, Salem Methodist Church at the corner of 127th Street was the largest and best-known church on Seventh Avenue. Near 134th Street was the popular Smalls' Paradise, one of the oldest nightclubs on Seventh Avenue.

James Van Der Zee, Harlem's most famous photographer, who documented so many famous Harlemites, had a studio on Seventh Avenue.

Exterior of the Hotel Theresa, 1950s. *Courtesy of David Goldman.*

Across the street from the Hotel Theresa on the northwest corner was African Memorial National Bookstore. Owners Willis Huggins and Lewis Micheaux were left-wing ideologues and their voluminous stock reflected their philosophy. W. E. B. Du Bois, Paul Robeson, A. Philip Randolph, and Thurgood Marshall were among the bookstore's regular customers. "If we couldn't find a book anywhere else," a customer of the National Bookstore said, "we always knew that Micheaux had a copy on hand; but perhaps more important than the availability of books was the kind of books he had—books on Africa now out of print; books on the history of us."

The Diamond Jewelry Store was next to the bookstore. "It was a front for the Mafia," recalled a former hotel resident. "It was the biggest numbers drop in Harlem. There was dope there. They sold jewelry as a cover. Lots of us from the hotel used to buy jewelry there. They never got raided. The police had to know what was going on. On Saturday nights, all these black cars would be lined up outside—nothing but white men going inside." Billy Rowe, the *Pittsburgh Courier* columnist, was talking about the gangsters who ran the Diamond Jewelry Store when he said, "The boys who electrify the corner are reduced to shiveling cowards whenever the Eastside torpedoes resplendent in their Brooks business suits descend upon Harlem to make their collections."

"You didn't place no quarter bet at the Jewelry Store," said longtime Harlemite Jake McKnight. "That was a place for big money. It wasn't small-time nickel-and-dime stuff. None of that was happening over there. The high rollers placed bets there."

"When the riots broke out in Harlem in 1964, nobody touched the Jewelry Store," said Harlem historian Preston Wilcox. "Everybody knew who controlled the place."

Brothers Morgan and Marvin Smith opened their first studio in 1939. The M. Smith Photo Studio was located at 243 West 125th Street, in the building next door to the Apollo Theater. The Kentucky-born photographers documented a visual history of countless legendary African-Americans and momentous Harlem milestones for nearly thirty years. By the late 1940s, the Smith brothers had a new neighbor in Romare Bearden, who taught art classes in the same building.

Adam Clayton Powell Jr. established the *People's Voice,* a weekly newspaper, in 1942. Located at 210 West 125th Street, the paper's aim was to smash stereotypes about black people and to encourage them to become more active in politics. The paper folded in 1948, three years after Powell was elected to Congress.

The old, dilapidated sign of the Blumstein's Department Store reminds a number of Harlemites of the store once called the "uptown Saks Fifth Avenue." "Blumstein's was the finest department store in Harlem," recalled businessman Nick Jones. "Not many blacks in Harlem went below 125th Street to shop."

Blumstein's was a few doors away from the hotel. Founded by brothers Jack and Kyver Blumstein in 1886, it was the largest department store in Harlem. A number of Harlemites remember the communitywide "don't buy where you can't work" campaign led by Adam Clayton Powell Jr. in the mid-1930s. Blumstein's was the target of an eight-week boycott because blacks were hired only in menial positions for insufficient wages. As the result of the protests, management reluctantly hired blacks as salespersons, but only those blacks who could pass for white.

"I worked at Blumstein's," recalled Naidine Collins. "That was my first job when I came to New York. That was in 1942. There were no dark-skinned blacks there when I worked there. At least not salespeople. The darker blacks were running the elevators and working as janitors."

Another series of boycotts ensued, led by the rabid Communist Party leader Benjamin Davis. By the late 1940s, if one walked into Blumstein's, there would have been blacks of all hues working side by side with white employees. At Christmastime, a black Santa was in the window adorned with black mannequins.

By 1953, Jack Blumstein said, "The employment policy at Blumstein's is one of the best in the city; turnover is slow with employees whose service ranges from five to thirty years. They are of all races and creeds, serving positions on every level."

In 1958, Martin Luther King Jr. was autographing copies of his first book, *Stride Toward Freedom*, at Blumstein's. "Suddenly, a deranged woman ran up and started screaming that he was a Communist and was trying to convert her to Catholicism," said Harlem emcee Hal Jackson, who was with King. "Without warning, she pulled a letter opener out of her pocket and plunged it into his chest."

Bobby "Happy Times" Robinson owns a record shop on 125th Street near Eighth Avenue that opened in 1946. Robinson, a slight man in his seventies, said, "I used to walk the streets to get ideas. I used to make it a point to walk the streets around four-thirty or five in the morning—often. I loved to watch the people sitting on their stoops, talking; I'd listen to the winos and their conversation, catch the whores on the street, listen to them talking to their pimps. I'd walk under the el when it was dark. I wouldn't dare now! It's a goddamn shame! I've got the oldest black business on the street. I've been here since the 1940s."

By the early 1940s, virtually every every white establishment on 125th Street was integrated except Frank's Restaurant, near Eighth Avenue. Beautiful palm trees adorned Frank's windows to offer its white clientele a degree of privacy while dining. Famous for steaks and seafood, the Greek-owned restaurant was the most elegant dining facility in Harlem. Frank's permitted certain black celebrities but, in general, maintained their Jim Crow policy until the late 1940s. There are a number of accounts of how blacks in the hotel reacted to Frank's Jim Crow policy.

"Joe Louis integrated Frank's Restaurant," recalled Preston Wilcox. "Joe called up from the Theresa and said I'm coming down to the restaurant, and I'm bringing some people with me. He made reservations. Joe was bold. Nobody was going to mess with the champ. Joe and his entourage went to Frank's. They were seated and nothing was said."

There is another version on who integrated Frank's: In 1940, a Jack Benny movie, *Buck Benny Rides Again,* premiered at the Loews Theater on 125th Street, which was one block from the Theresa. Rochester (Anderson) had a starring role in the movie. While in New York, Rochester stayed in the Theresa. After leaving Loews, Rochester and his entourage headed to Frank's Restaurant.

"There was Rochester and his people, a few press guys, and a few of us behind the press group," recalled former Theresa employee Horace Carter. "Rochester boldly walked into Frank's. We all followed him. I was thinking—we are going to be thrown out of the damn place. But the waiters realized who Rochester was and gave us all menus. I think they were afraid of Jack Benny so they weren't going to mess with Rochester. After that night, Frank's let blacks come in."

"Grace Nail Johnson integrated Frank's," said Naidine Collins. "She was light enough to pass for white and did pass whenever she wanted to. In the early 1940s, she took a group of black people from the Theresa to Frank's and ordered steaks for everybody. They served her party. That's the first time that I recall any black people getting service in Frank's. And the next day, everybody in the Theresa was talking about it. After that, Frank's only let light-skinned blacks in like Willie Bryant and Adam Clayton Powell Jr. Black people had to be damn near white to get in."

"Grace Johnson had experience walking into the best restaurants in downtown New York," recalled Jewel Sims Okala. "Frank's certainly wasn't a problem. There was no business in all of New York that she wouldn't enter. In 1942, our brownstone on Seventh Avenue caught fire. While it was being repaired, Grace, my husband, and I moved into suites 721 and 723 in the Theresa. In fact, my wedding reception dinner was held in the hotel's dining room a few months before we moved there. My husband was French-Nigerian—neither of us could pass for white. I'd dress like an Indian and put a red dot on my forehead. My husband wore his native-African attire. We'd get a car and head downtown to Le Cirque's or one of the other expensive establishments. Grace didn't walk in and say, 'I'm white.' She just went wherever she wanted to go and that was that. They knew Grace because she was a regular customer. They thought she was a rich white lady. The waiters assumed my husband and I were foreigners. When we walked in, two or three waiters descended upon us. They were so gracious to my husband and me. We often spoke French in their presence. Grace wanted to make the point that racism was irrational. White folks back then would serve anybody but an American Negro."

Two

A PLACE TO UNITE

The Hotel Theresa was integrated at a time when most downtown hotels wouldn't accept blacks. If they were allowed to stay downtown, they suffered such indignities as having to use the back entrance to theaters and clubs they were playing and couldn't sit down at the bar for a drink afterward. Room service was a requirement because white management didn't want blacks visible. To understand the significance of the Hotel Theresa to the Harlem community, and to African-Americans everywhere, we need more than a vague notion of the burden that Jim Crow imposed.

Few in Harlem remember the well-publicized snub Josephine Baker, the black diva of France, received in the Stork Club. The buzz that hit the press was that all the young fashionistas residing in the Theresa were practically giddy silly while rushing about putting their best threads in order to wear to the Roxy Theater where the international star and rage of Paris, Josephine Baker, was appearing. Gossips in the Theresa's club room and mezzanine were all chattering about Baker's $250,000 Paris wardrobe that had been designed especially for her Roxy performance. On October 16, 1951, after Baker performed her usual song stylings and exotic dancing at the Roxy, Broadway performer Roger Rico and his wife, Solange, made

Josephine Baker. *Photograph by John W. Mosley. Courtesy of the Charles L. Blockson Afro-American Collection, Temple University.*

reservations for a late-night dinner at the Stork Club, and they invited Josephine Baker and former showgirl-turned-politician Bessie Buchanan.

Bessie Buchanan insisted that Baker should join her and the Ricos. "You are French, Josephine," Buchanan insisted, as if Josephine's French citizenship would inoculate her from racism. Baker's friend and singer Thelma Carpenter questioned Buchanan's motives. Carpenter had an inkling that Buchanan was up to something and insisted to Josephine that she was being used by the backstabbing Buchanan. Bessie had persuaded the Ricos to invite Baker to the Stork Club because she knew there would likely be trouble. Buchanan knew that her light complexion would enable her to pass for white, but that would not be the case for Baker. Buchanan had her eye on politics, and a racist snub against an international celebrity like Baker would make good campaign material for Harlem voters, whom she intended to represent as New York State assemblywoman. "Josephine had done her last show, she was sitting with a hat on her head, naked except for a Hermès scarf tied around her belly like an apron," recalled Thelma Carpenter. "She said she was going to the Stork Club. I told her not to take Bessie: I said, 'It's trouble.'" Bessie's husband, Charles Buchanan, manager of the Savoy Ballroom, even admitted that Bessie had contrived the entire evening. She prompted the Ricos to set up the event and invite her and Baker. "I spent over four hundred thousand dollars on my wife's political ambitions, just so I could have some peace," said Charlie Buchanan. Dressed in a royal blue silk gown and her hair in a long ponytail hanging to her waist, the forty-five-year-old Josephine was feeling unusually hungry when the party arrived at the Stork Club after midnight. They ordered a round of drinks and were served. When dinner was ordered, Baker requested steak and a bottle of red vintage wine. The Stork Club was usually crowded and orders typically took a while. As time passed, Baker became anxious. "When my husband called the waiters, they acted as if they didn't hear him," recalled Solange Rico. "Finally one waiter came to the table and said there were no steaks left. Then my husband asked for crab cakes. None of them were left either. 'Very well,' said my husband, 'we are going to order something else.' But the waiter was already gone." The refusal of service went straight to the boss himself, Stork Club owner Sherman Billingsley, who had passed Josephine Baker. After a double take, he'd asked, "Who the fuck let her in?" Word was soon passed by the waiters: "No service for the Baker table."

Stories about the Josephine Baker–Stork Club incident filled the Harlem newspapers for weeks, with Bessie Buchanan at the center. Stories in the *New York Amsterdam News* in particular, moved activists in the Theresa Hotel like Anna Arnold Hedgeman, Bessie Buchanan, Walter White, and Willie Bryant to put on their marching shoes and picket in front of the celebrated nightclub. Carrying signs like "Famous Nite Spot Just a White Spot," picketers were both vocal and impassioned in their protest of the club's racism. One night, Duke Ellington's sister, Ruth Ellington James, and the cast members from *South Pacific* and *Guys and Dolls* joined the picket line.

Radio personality Walter Winchell was in the Stork Club the night of the incident. Baker accused him of not intervening on her behalf. Winchell, a founder of the Damon Runyon Cancer Fund, as was Sugar Ray Robinson, said that he was "appalled by their efforts to involve me in an incident in which I had no part."

Back at the Theresa, Robinson was telling friends that he was not quitting the Runyon fund as a consequence of this now public scandal. He argued that Baker had created the problem and she was being unfair to Winchell, and he (Robinson) dodged the heat from his peers by leaving town.

In an interview, Baker disagreed with a reporter who suggested that the incident had bearing only on the 14 million African-Americans. "This is something which involves every fair-minded American," she said. "It's a matter of democracy and justice which could affect anyone caught in the tentacles of discrimination and prejudice."

As late as 1956, the National Association of Fashion and Accessories Design tried to book a banquet room at the Stork Club to host a show featuring black models. When the press got wind of the show, they assumed that the Stork Club's Billingsley would try to vindicate himself from the Baker incident. But days before the show, he canceled the booking, telling reporters, "They can go to hell."

Two years after the Baker Stork Clubs incident, Bessie Buchanan stood outside the doors of the Theresa Hotel to announce her candidacy for the New York State Assembly. A former Cotton Club showgirl, she became the first black female to serve in the State Senate. "Bessie could sell herself," recalled dancer Hycie Curtis. "Even in show business, she couldn't do a damn thing, but she always got a spot. I figure Bessie gave Josephine bad advice. She knew what would happen."

But the Stork Club incident had not been Baker's first experience with racist white proprietors. A 1941 Pittsburgh *Courier* article reported in "The American way of life is working its strange pattern on Josephine Baker; she and her French husband [Jo Bouillion] are finding it difficult to secure hotel reservations in the better spots in the lower Manhattan jungle."

The cruel reality of Jim Crow for black people in New York City was difficult to swallow. New York City had represented the promised land to the legions of black people who had abandoned the segregated South and to those who remained. In a town presumably as liberal as New York, with its swank hotels, hip nightspots, chic restaurants, and world-class museums, its rigid bigotry seem bizarre. If an international superstar like Josephine Baker wasn't welcome downtown, then who would be?

Judge James Watson, who frequented the Theresa Hotel in the 1940s and 1950s, expressed that: "We [blacks] really didn't want to go downtown. We had a luxurious hotel now and the burden of being rejected and despised was lifted." Former *Pittsburgh Courier* columnist Evelyn Cunningham said, "Nothing can compensate you for being turned away at a downtown hotel. So you didn't go there."

In a 1947 column, Billy Rowe was thinking about bigotry in downtown New York when he wrote, "There are those who would rather still be a lamppost in New York than the mayor of some nice little thriving [Southern] town. However, there are a lot of happenings here that leave this parade watcher plenty ashamed of his citizenship heritage. In a town supposed as democratic as this one, nightclub, hotel, and restaurant bigotry is so hard to take."

When orchestra leader Jimmie Lunceford died of a heart attack in 1947, his final experience in life was the disgrace of racism. "The band was on the road. We were in Seaside, Oregon, in 1947," recalled trumpet player Joe Wilder. "The band stopped at a Portland,

Oregon, restaurant expecting to eat. We couldn't get any service. But all the other white folks were eating. They said they were closing. The next I knew the police were in the place. We left. Jimmie had a heart attack an hour later. For a long time after that night, I thought about that incident in the restaurant. It was his last experience on earth. We always gathered at the Theresa when our band went on tour. And that's where the bus put us off when we returned. When we got back to the Theresa after Jimmie's death, we all felt so much better. There was a lot of crying and hugging because being in that hotel surrounded by all those black people who loved Jimmie made us feel so much better. That Oregon experience, I won't forget because it still reminds me of Jimmie's death."

Bandleaders Joe Thomas and Ed Wilcox took over Jimmie Lunceford's orchestra. Billy Rowe told his readers in the *Pittsburgh Courier* that the orchestra retained its "rhythmic sting and sing which first found it a smooth path on the road to glory."

Joe Louis's wife, Marva Trotter, suffered the indignities of racial discrimination during her short-lived singing career. "Well, what I started out to say is that Marva made her grand opening at the Ebony Club on Broadway," said Joe Louis. "She kept at it for a good while, but her manager told her she needed more experience to build up her voice and booked her on a bunch of one-night stands through the South. Marva got herself a chauffeur and set out to conquer the world. But after three months on the road, having to go to the back door of restaurants to get her food, eating and sleeping in the car, she gave up. I was glad about that. It's degrading for a woman who's had the best to be told, 'Go round the back.' "

Joe Louis's concern for his wife was due to his own numerous encounters with racism. He was subjected to insults even as the world boxing champion when he joined the segregated army to defend his nation. While traveling on the Norfolk ferry in the mid-1940s, the champ, without thinking, tried to purchase a magazine from the whites-only waiting room. A white menial worker hurled profanities at him.

"I remember visiting Billy Eckstine while he was on tour in the South," recalled the writer Jack Schiffman. "It was before he was to appear at a dance. His dressing room was the bus! There he was, earning more money than the president of the United States, and he was changing his clothes on a bus. He wasn't the first black entertainer to note the irony."

No matter how hostile the racial climate in most of America at the time, the Theresa's doors were always open to African-Americans, allowing them to feel a sense of security behind her walls. The hotel was black America's haven—its sanctuary. Rhythm and blues singer Chuck Jackson came to the hotel the first time in 1953 at the age of nineteen. His songs "I Don't Want to Cry" and "Everybody Needs Love" made him one of the most sought-after singers by the early 1960s.

"When my band toured in the South, we couldn't stay in hotels," said Chuck. "We often slept in rooming houses or sometimes we slept in our cars. But we were always eager to get back to New York. When we saw people who were going to be in New York, we'd say, 'Meet me at the Theresa.' We knew we would stay there and it gave us a sense of security. We loved being with other blacks. We could relax because we didn't have to deal with racism. There was a solidarity among blacks who gathered in the hotel—a kind of solidarity that we don't have today. And I doubt if we will ever have a place like the Theresa again.

"I was staying in the Theresa working on some songs and couldn't pay my rent. Charles Rangel was desk clerk at the time. I was a few weeks behind. Didn't have any money to catch up. When I walked into the lobby, Charles Rangel would have his head down. He pretended to be reading the newspaper so it appeared that he didn't see me when I passed him. No white person would have looked after me like that. I saw him a few years ago and reminded him about those days and we had a good laugh."

Sammy Davis Jr., oddly enough, was one black performer who refused to stay at the Theresa. When he and Nat King Cole played the Copacabana, Nat went uptown to the Theresa. Sammy opted out. He had a different notion about his hotel accommodations and said, "They [blacks] haven't made a hotel that's luxurious as I want to live in." When he performed at the Copacabana or other downtown clubs, he resided at the exclusive Sherry Netherlands around the corner from the club. Often, he checked into the Waldorf-Astoria "or wherever anyone else with my fame and financial ability would be able to stay," he said.

"In the Theresa's heyday," said writer Tony Scherman, "it sparkled a stylish response to an ugly reality—the Jim Crow policy of the big Midtown hotels. A brown-skinned visitor to New York who wanted good accommodations stayed at the Theresa. It was that simple."

For the majority of blacks, the ascendance of the Hotel Theresa was regarded as a sign that they had finally arrived, at least on Seventh Avenue and 125th Street. The Theresa's rooms, her bar, her restaurants, her swank shops, were home to all black comers—and they came through the front door. It was a sanctuary for affluent blacks from around the world. So if segregation meant the Theresa was the only place that blacks felt welcome, then the upside to this Jim Crow treatment was that blacks had a place to unite. The riches of the black world were under one roof rather than scattered throughout Manhattan. And the wannabes could be near the famous.

Three

THE SIDEWALK CAPTAINS

The ingenious Billy Rowe had begun writing for the *Pittsburgh Courier* in 1940 and made titillating gossip about the Hotel Theresa's patrons the centerpiece of his column, which was read nationwide. The showbiz heavyweights generated sensational stories in and around the Theresa. When the hotel opened its doors to blacks in 1940, Rowe seized this opportunity to make a name for himself by becoming the most famous chronicler of the hotel in its heyday. His syndicated column in the *Courier* provided the link from the goings-on inside the Theresa Hotel to blacks in urban environs and to those in the backwoods and canebrake. People who could only dream of being in the hotel felt a spirit of family for the famous whom they had come to know through Billy Rowe's column.

"I would call Billy Rowe an ingenious hustler," said the writer Jean Booker. "I say that because he became a deputy police commissioner without having been a policeman. That happened because he was approved by the black politicians in Harlem and the white politicians who controlled them from Tammany Hall. (Rowe was appointed deputy police commissioner after he left the *Pittsburgh Courier,* in 1953.) Adam Clayton Powell Jr. was the first black Harlem politician who was independent. No one controlled him. They tried. He did exactly what the

Ophelia DeVore (*second from right*), Billy Rowe (*third from right*), and Beah Richards (*fourth from right*) with unidentified persons in the Hotel Theresa's dining room, 1950s. *Courtesy of Ophelia DeVore.*

white politicians did. That's why he was so hated by the white establishment. That's why he had to be brought down."

In response to the outcry over Rowe's appointment, a *New York Amsterdam News* editorial reported. "We are, to put it mildly, greatly disappointed that no Negro policemen were elevated to higher positions." Harlem was the desired place to be a policeman, especially the 123rd Precinct. "It was a gold mine," said writer Helen Lawrenson. "In fact, some cops even paid kickbacks to be seconded to that locality. They got paid off by pimps, whores, numbers runners and bankers, bars, nightclubs, everyone. Not only the cops but also higher police officials and many judges."

"It wasn't just that precinct," said musician Danny Moore. "It was all over New York."

When he became a deputy police commissioner, Rowe certainly knew where every numbers drop was located in Harlem. And he had written about the bankers and the drop locations in his column. He knew who the major numbers bankers were, such as his good friends Chink Cunningham and Johnny Walker, who were underlings for mobsters Dutch Schultz and Lucky Luciano. These major underworld figures attended Billy Rowe's farewell party when he left the *Courier*.

"In those days, you talk about mixing it up," said Marjorie Corbitt, a longtime Harlem resident. "When there are no jobs, you can't discriminate. So many people in Harlem were tied to the underworld indirectly or directly. I knew numbers bankers who were married to teachers and nurses."

"My husband, Chink Cunningham, a major numbers banker, paid for my master's degree at Columbia," said Evelyn Cunningham.

In a *Courier* column called "Billy Rowe's Notebook," Rowe revealed hair-raising stories about the stars and other celebrities. Rowe dished on who was cavorting with whom, which couples were headed for divorce court, and who was engaging in chicanery. He exposed the nodders on the needles, the sexual escapades of the "beige" chorus girls, who signed record and movie deals, who got good reviews, and who was broke.

Rowe wrote a 1942 column, for example, declaring that the Pennsylvania case against June Eckstine, the wife of crooner Billy Eckstine, for molesting a female minor, was thrown out of court. Mrs. Eckstine was represented by Raymond Pace Alexander, an African-American, Harvard-trained lawyer. "Raymond Pace Alexander, who was in there pitching all the time, gets the win," wrote Rowe. "June and her crooning Billy are still as close as twelve o'clock and taking their mail out of the same box."

"What Billy didn't write," about the sexual escapades of the famous, said Danny Moore, "was that so much of that stuff was going on in the Theresa Hotel. It was Billy Eckstine's fault the way I see it. He and a lot of those famous men encouraged their wives to include another female sex partner. When the men had to hit the road for a gig, the women went at it without them. I don't see that it was a big deal." The accusations certainly didn't appear to have created conflict enough to destroy the Eckstine union. A few years later, Rowe was writing about the Eckstines again: "The Billy Eckstines patched up their family misunderstanding before anybody had a chance to gloat over the split."

Rowe's column read like a sensational soap opera with a cast of characters that included society matrons, intellectuals, sporting guys, bandleaders, and the showgirls—all the stylers and profilers onstage at Seventh Avenue and 125th Street. Anyone in show business wanted to be in Billy Rowe's column—even his best friend, Joe Louis. "Not even the heavy betting boys have made up their minds as to just who will be the victor June 18 [1942] when Louis and Conn makes with the mad," wrote Billy. "But an even bet will get you anything, except a room, that it will be a sure defeat for [manager] Walter W. Scott of the Theresa Hotel. If he had twice as many rooms, he wouldn't be able to lodge all the folk who have been trying for more than a year to sleep and be seen there during the fight."

Three weeks following the fight, the wife of bandleader Lucky Millinder, a year-round resident of the Theresa, was a subject of Rowe's column. Sally Nix Millinder refused to identify herself as black or white, and Rowe wanted to know why. He reported that when Sally took her children to Atlantic City, a white lady near the boardwalk called them "niggers" and Sally caused a near riot.

"I met her brothers," recalled Naidine Collins. "They looked white to me. I'm certain they identified themselves as white. Sally loved to play that race game. No one understood why Sally wouldn't say if she was black or white. When her husband, Lucky Millinder, drove her to Texas where she came from, the Klan put one beating on Lucky down there. They tried to kill him for driving down South in a fancy car with a white woman. I don't know how Lucky got out of that alive."

Rowe used his column to create light-hearted dissension. Such as the time he wrote, "That society young man brushed up that very stacked girl from Norristown in the Theresa Hotel the other ayem because she said no, is engaged to a girl who should find him out before saying 'I do.' "

The Theresa was home to Billy Rowe because the *Courier* offices were across the street from the hotel on Seventh Avenue. From his windows, Rowe could see who was coming and going into the hotel. Largely because of his ability to tap into the Theresa's gossip, the *Courier* had the largest circulation among black weekly newspapers published between both world wars of the twentieth century. In addition to Pittsburgh, the *Courier* published editions in New York, Chicago, Los Angeles, Philadelphia, New Orleans, Kansas City, Little Rock, and Detroit.

Through his public relations skills and quick-witted tactics, Rowe amassed a stockpile of important Hollywood friends like Darryl Zanuck, Louis B. Mayer, and Orson Welles who gave him access to the gossip in the movie industry. Rowe understood his own power and used it to promote himself socially and financially.

A few who remember him said he had a big ego. He was a dapper dresser who craved compliments. Tall, deep brown, and handsome, Rowe sported a fedora that was his trademark. When he walked into the *Courier* offices, somebody had better hurry up and tell him that he looked good. He was notoriously cheap too. He thought his presence was enough to substitute for the check at the Theresa bar. People who wanted to get into his column stuck envelopes stuffed with cash under his door at the *Courier* office. Billy Rowe was so powerful nobody would cross him.

"Billy was vindictive if someone disagreed with him," recalled Evelyn Cunningham, a fellow *Courier* writer. "He wasn't vindictive in the way that Walter Winchell was. Winchell tried to ruin his enemies. Billy ignored them. That was painful for them because if a celebrity got a lucrative movie contract, or a major record deal, nothing about it ever appeared in his column. That's how he showed his contempt for them. He wasn't a lovable man. But everybody loved his wife, Isadora, whom we affectionately called Izzy."

"There was a great deal of vanity in Billy," said his cousin

Frazelle Williams. "He lied about his age. Billy was born in South Carolina. He was an only child. He came to New York as a young boy—maybe ten years old. He was older than he claimed to be by four years. He and Izzy didn't have much if anything to do with me and my family. I didn't get to know him until a few years before he died in 1997. He and Izzy lived a lifestyle that put them in a circle with Sammy Davis Jr., Joe Louis, Lena Horne, Billy Eckstine—Billy knew them all. They went to the big parties and entertained a lot of important big shots in their home. I wasn't invited. When Billy got sick and needed some help, I was there for him."

"Now, Billy was a smart guy," said Joe Louis. "Dressed real sharp, and good-looking. Everybody in Harlem knew him, and he had all kinds of commendations from civic groups."

A number of Rowe's best scoops came from his informants who hung around the hotel where they spied on the rich and famous. Billy called his spies the "big town boys" and the "sidewalk captains." His informants made sure he had all the hot stories and the juicy tips they could dig up on the showbiz crowd, other residents of the hotel, and those from the wider black community. The hotel was always buzzing with hot rumors, and Billy's spies did a lot of digging there.

Willie Bryant, a year-round resident of the Theresa, was one of Rowe's zealous informants. Bryant had secretly married and divorced Edna Mae Holly years before she became Mrs. Sugar Ray Robinson. Without mentioning that they were married, in a 1941 column Billy said, "Edna Mae Holly may think twice and not leave Willie Bryant to go show touring with Cab Calloway, whose radio quizzical is just a jump ahead of a commercial and is being billed among the outstanding radio programs of the day."

Edna Mae Robinson never admitted that she was married to

Willie Bryant. She often said, "Why are people saying that I was married to that man?"

Bryant appeared to be an unlikely candidate for a gossip given his own impressive credentials. The New Orleans native was one of the most sought-after black deejays in New York. Tall, slim, "hawk-nosed," and intelligent, he looked like Adam Clayton Powell Jr. He worked with Ralph Cooper as an Apollo emcee for a number of years. He was the male lead opposite Ethel Waters in the smash Broadway hit *Mamba's Daughter*. He used his high-powered contacts in the entertainment community on both coasts to help numbers of young blacks to get into show business. Bryant succeeded Bill "Bojangles" Robinson as "unofficial" mayor of Harlem after Robinson's death in 1949. Bryant was an emcee at the Baby Grand on radio channel WHOM. He "loved to call out the names of the hot babes in the Hotel Theresa where he lived," said Billy Rowe. Bryant's female listeners in the hotel stayed up past midnight hoping to hear their names called on air. Bryant worked with Nipsey Russell, who was, at that time, a showman at the Baby Grand.

"Willie Bryant was a nice man—generous," recalled hotel messenger Horace Carter. "Everybody loved Willie. He was down-to-earth. That's why he was so beloved."

Not everyone remembers Willie Bryant fondly. Naidine Collins recalled Bryant this way: "When I first met him I liked him fine. So many people said he was a great guy. When I first came to the Theresa, I had a friend who was in high school. I had just graduated myself. So she was only one or two years younger than me. Whenever she came to the hotel we went out to the movies or shopping. One day, we were in the lobby. It was a school day. She was out of school for some reason. So she came by the hotel to visit me. Willie Bryant came up to us. He looked at me and said, 'No wonder I can't get next to you. You've got your piece here.' He was referring to my high school friend. That really hurt me because there was nothing like that going on between us. I knew that he would spread the story. That's what he did around the hotel. Gossiped. His wife, Pat, was very nice. Whenever she washed her hair, I used to sit for hours combing her long wavy hair dry on the hotel's fire escape outside their suite."

Pee Wee Marquette idolized Billy Rowe. Marquette spent every moment he could spare under the hotel marquee listening for rumors in the grapevine. He was a well-known emcee at Smalls' Paradise and lived in the Braddock Hotel on 126th Street and Eighth Avenue.

"Pee Wee was so tiny," recalled a former resident of the hotel. "He came up to my waist. I was five feet five inches tall in those days. I've shrunk with age. It's not like he was a dwarf—he was a midget. His arm, legs, hands, were like a tiny five- or six-year-old child's. He could be the nicest person. He was very talkative and friendly one day. Then the next day, he could turn into a real bastard. He'd argue with someone who came and stood in his favorite spot on the sidewalk—something so simple could set him off. Pee Wee had the filthiest mouth. If Maceo [Birch] or Willie [Bryant] tried to reason with him—calm him down—he'd curse them out too. He used curse words that I'd never heard. One day, he got into a loud argument with Bill [Bojangles] Robinson who was always telling darky jokes. Pee Wee didn't like Robinson's jokes. They got into it. Robinson had a bad temper too. So that got pretty loud."

"Pee Wee had girls too. As small as he was, there were women in the hotel who were interested in him," recalled a former showgirl who knew Pee Wee. "It was for his money. Many women didn't have money in those days. Some women would do anything to feed their kids or feed themselves, even if it meant being with Pee Wee. There wasn't any work in Harlem. Pee Wee was too tiny for anybody to be serious about him in that way."

"I never saw Pee Wee with women. The stories were that he was really a girl," said Danny Moore. "That's the way I heard it. All that aside, he was one of the best emcees around. Certainly, he was one of the most popular in his day. You can't mention the Birdland Club without mentioning Pee Wee Marquette. He was the emcee there also. He did the usual—introduced the bands and so forth. He was a drawing card too. He was hired to attract people because of his tiny size—he was used like a freak, a gimmick. Pee Wee brought Billy Rowe all the news from the Birdland nightspot."

"Willie Bryant and Pee Wee used their positions as emcees to hustle recording artists," recalled longtime Harlem resident Marjorie Corbitt. "They shook down the singers in those days. They'd play their records more than they ordinarily would have in exchange for money. That wasn't legal."

Radarman was another source of gossip for Billy Rowe. Radarman was a two-bit hustler who had earned that nickname by getting dirt on celebrities. He was light-skinned, tall, and skinny. Radarman was eventually killed by another hustler.

"Radar knew everything that was going on inside the hotel," recalled Naidine Collins. "If you wanted some information on somebody in the hotel, or anybody in Harlem, Radarman could find out. Nothing got past him. He lived up on St. Nicholas Avenue and 145th Street. Radar got some juicy stories that were too hot for Billy Rowe to print. He told us that Edna Mae Robinson [Sugar Ray's wife] was going with Althea Gibson. Both Ray and Edna had befriended Althea—treated her like family. Radar said the reason Ray and Edna

Mae fought constantly was because he was always catching Edna Mae with other women. Radar told us about Dinah Washington—I think it was husband number three. She married about six or seven times, so I can't remember which one. Each husband got younger. She cut his clothes off with a razor blade in the Theresa. Whew! Dinah was something else. It didn't take much to set her off. Dinah used to give some wild parties in the Theresa. She could cuss like a sailor. When Dinah threw her parties, Pee Wee Marquette used to sit on her lap like a baby while her guests looked on in amazement."

Maceo Birch came to New York from Kansas City, Missouri. He was a fervent gossip and a small-time con artist who never paid for anything, not even his room in the Hotel Theresa. He lived in the hotel year-round. His rent tab was paid by Willie Bryant most of the time. Birch had a reputation for being a deadbeat. Maceo bragged to others in the hotel that he didn't pay for his room, his food or his drinks. He said as long as others paid, he never intended to pay for anything. Three times a year, he traveled from Harlem to the West Coast. He'd stop in his native Kansas City, then head to Detroit and Chicago. While in those cities, he penetrated the grapevine to get the juice for Billy Rowe's column. When Birch returned to his usual spot in front of the hotel, Rowe made certain that his readers were informed of "the Birch's" return and the juicy stories he'd scooped. Rowe couldn't resist tantalizing his readers after another Birch adventure. "Just when the guys and gals had given Maceo Birch up for lost he returned from his cross-country jaunt with an imagination full of tales about the habitants of the eye-men corners from here to the sunkissed shores. The sidewalk captains outside the Theresa were enlivened and surprised at the return to their league of Maceo Birch.

All the regulars were on hand to hear his tales of the former New Yorkers he encountered across the nation. Birch was shocked, however, to find that it was even a hassle to find a curb clerk to take a number or two. The center of attraction these days among the sidewalk office-holder afront the Theresa Hotel, the Birch that isn't bark, holds the concrete for hours. Said he saw so many people he could almost write a book, but decided to settle for just a column. After talking with him for hours with Major Robinson [of the *Chicago Defender*] taking mental notes, it was discovered that even his minute memory had failed to record whether it was true or false. He has the avenue abuzz as all of the sportsmen, socialites, celebrities, slickers, playboys, and politicians in town for the Joe Louis championship battle, are whispering the possible re-marriage of Joe and Marva. Most bets are that they will again be Mr. and Mrs. if the telephone bills between the Theresa and the West Coast are any indication."

During one of Birch's trips to Los Angeles in 1948, he found that the most asked-about New Yorkers were nightclub owner Red Randolph, Willie Bryant, Adam Clayton Powell Jr. and wife Hazel Scott (whom Rowe said was Harlem's best-dressed beauty), international gambler Finley Hoskins, the glamorous showgirls Tondeleyo, and twin sisters Hibbie and Hazel Brown. He saw former Theresa resident Billy Kenny of the Ink Spots. He learned that Kenny and his wife were divorcing.

"The twins, Hibbie and Hazel Brown, were in the life—you know," said former barmaid Ruth Guzzman. "They ran around with the sporting guys. When they hit town in the forties, they were the talk of the Harlem because they were so beautiful. One of them did luck up and marry a doctor. That's how she got out of the life."

"Maceo was average height with golden brown skin," recalled a hotel resident. "I used to touch his face whenever I left the hotel. I'd say to him, 'You've got the prettiest skin.' He was a New York City greeter. A greeter meant that if a lady was coming to New York from California or any city and she didn't know anyone, Maceo would make sure she had a nice room in the hotel with a good view. He got tickets to shows. He'd escort her around town during her visit. When men came to New York, the greeters made sure they had accommodations and lined up girls for them. There were some others in the hotel who were greeters. Being a New York City greeter was a big deal. Escorts entertained the wealthiest black and sometimes white people from across the country. Benjamin Mays and Jesse Owens used escorts when they came to New York."

"Maceo Birch was friendly with Miss DeLaney," recalled former Theresa employee Debbie McDade, "She was a teacher from Raleigh, North Carolina. She came to the Theresa every summer. Miss DeLaney went out with a lot of different men. Lots of men were in and out of her room. We used to whisper about her because everybody said that she was such a prude down in Raleigh. But when she came to the Theresa, she was on the wild side. She had prominent relatives in New York. But we never saw them in the hotel."

Rowe gave the sidewalk captains plenty of ink in his column, especially Willie Bryant and Maceo Birch. The two informants were so familiar to his readers that they were national celebrities. "Willie Bryant is paying a lot of attention to the mail man these days as he's expecting a very rich legacy any day," Rowe told his readers. In a spring 1947 column, he was paying attention to race matters when he wrote: "WOR called in Willie Bryant to audition for that all-nite record spot. We thought at last the barriers there would bite the dust and he would break through. . . . Seems so funny that the FEPC of this state has failed to dig into radio discrimination." Rowe called attention to Bryant again when he wrote that "talk at the Theresa bar is that former chorus girl and now movie starlet Francine Everett is in need of a male lead for her upcoming role in Irwin C. Miller's *Brown-skinned Models*. The bar hangers are cracking up as Willie Bryant and Ralph Cooper seem to be gearing up to apply for the role."

Rowe also enjoyed poking fun at the sidewalk captains. In a 1946 column, he wrote, "Evelyn Sylvia Harding is back in town after that ovah time sojourn in Pittsburgh ravin' about the nice guys she met. That, of course, does not speak too well for the characters who hang around the Theresa Hotel."

Wheelers and dealers under the marquee were singing Rowe's praises when he tackled race discrimination again by answering the charges alleged by Walter Winchell in his column "New York's Black Magic." Winchell in a 1945 article promoted hate and misunderstanding when he referred to Harlem as a hovel of "prostitootsies and trouble makers which never stops to catch its breath."

Although Winchell's comments were symptomatic of America's troubling racial legacy, he was a powerful man of the media who had the ability to make racial stereotypes stick in the hearts and minds of countless white Americans. Winchell had to be countered. Rowe was cheered when he responded in his column that the conditions in Harlem were not created by its residents but by "invisible lines drawn by restrictive covenants . . . unwritten laws . . . and opportunity denials which snatch away the hope of our youth . . . whose fire and flare to go out and conquer the world are stifled early by racial discrimination and prejudice. Of course in Harlem we have rat infested tenements, breeding more slums than there should be. . . .

We have more unemployment than there is in your community, and a greater fight for life, liberty and the pursuit of human dignity."

A number of guests in the hotel had seen Darryl Zanuck's *No Way Out* at Loews Theater down the street from the Theresa. Rowe gave high praise to his friend Darryl Zanuck and 20th Century Fox for being on the cutting edge of movies with racial themes. Directed by Joseph Mankiewicz, *No Way Out* was made in 1950. Sidney Poitier was cast as a young doctor who has to choose between his medical oath to save lives or saving the life of a racist gangster played by Richard Widmark. Just a few years earlier, Poitier could be seen hanging out at the Palm Restaurant across from the hotel, or making deliveries to the hotel from his barbecue joint on 137th Street. Other cast members included Linda Darnell and Ruby Dee. Darryl Zanuck had made the movie *Pinky* in 1949. Directed by Elia Kazan, the cast includes Jeanne Crain, Ethel Barrymore, and Ethel Waters. *Pinky* was one of the most melodramatic movies ever produced about interracial romance and society's bigotry. Billy Rowe said that many white reviewers thought that *Pinky* had been enough from Zanuck on the question of race relations. In his typically entertaining style, Rowe suggested that his praise for Zanuck might concern a number of liberal whites and blacks who were afraid that his endorsement of *No Way Out* would stop other producers from making fair-minded pictures on race in America.

Billy Rowe longed for the big town boys and his exciting life in Harlem when he traveled. He amusingly shared his fantasy of life back at the hotel in a spring 1947 column: "When we get to the big town, a five will get you ten that Willie Bryant will still be holding down his usual cobbled spot afront the Theresa Hotel telling Maceo Birch, Neil Scott, or Dick Smythe about something funny that hap-

Duke Ellington playing the piano surrounded by musicians, 1940s. *Photograph by John W. Mosley. Courtesy of the Charles L. Blockson Afro-American Collection, Temple University.*

pened the night before during his record spinning chores. The all see-ing eyes of Pee Wee Marquette will be bulging just as much as ever every time a pretty face, running into a nice figure, passes in review before the 125th Street eatery . . . on the ground floor of the Theresa. Dan Burley will not have changed his say and will be running helter-skelter about the town bending the ears of all and sundry. . . . Sally Nix Millinder and her sister Cookie will be found, as usual, lithing in and out of the Theresa lobby, looking trim, well-pressed and pretty."

"When I traveled around the country on *Courier* business," re-called Evelyn Cunningham, "everyplace I went, people asked about the celebrities who stayed in the Theresa. Then they'd ask about Billy Rowe, Willie Bryant, Maceo Birch, Joe Louis, and Adam Clay-ton Powell. George Schuyler, Billy Rowe, and I were the top three re-porters in the *Courier*'s New York offices. But Billy got the most mail. A *Courier* study in the 1940s revealed that each issue was read by no less than fifteen people."

"When I was growing up in Norristown, Pennsylvania, everybody wanted to read the *Pittsburgh Courier*," recalled historian Charles L. Blockson. "There were people from Pennsylvania who lived in the Theresa or hung around the hotel. We were excited to read about them. We often knew them or their families. They were famous, so that was a thrill to read about them. We read Billy Rowe's column from the Philadelphia edition of the *Courier*. That was popular in my neighbor-hood. He wrote stories about June and Billy Eckstine—they were from Pennsylvania. June came from the Mainline. He wrote about the ac-tress Marion Bruce. Her family lived near us in those days. Then there was the actress Mildred Davenport, who called herself Acquanetta, an-other Pennsylvania native."

"I lived in Ohio in the 1940s, and we thought everybody who stayed at the Theresa was famous and had lots of money," said Susie H., who sold bootleg liquor and hot food in her home. "That's all my customers talked about when they gathered in my house on weekends. They wanted to talk about the Theresa. Some of the folks who couldn't read had the *Courier* read to them. Then some others who didn't want to know about nothing else in the paper—they just wanted to know what Billy Rowe had to say. The *Courier* was the most important black paper to read in those days. It was like the Bible. You didn't throw the *Courier* away."

"We couldn't afford to buy the *Courier* when I was a young woman in Arkansas," recalled former vaudeville actress KennerBelle Jackson. "My family waited for our neighbors to read it and pass it to us. Then we took it to church and gave it to someone there. They would pass it on. People couldn't wait to get their hands on Billy Rowe's column to read about the celebrities in the Theresa Hotel and those from other places.

"I was a ham actress by the mid-1940s. We called them medicine shows in those days. I was on the road a lot. The first thing I did when I got to the next town was to look for the colored library so I could get the *Courier*. When I could afford to buy a copy I used to clip Billy Rowe's column and send it to friends who couldn't get the *Courier*. I still have some of those old clippings around the house. I used to love to read about Rose Morgan and her beauty shops—the Rose Morgan look was in back then. There were very few things in our lives in those days that made us feel good . . . Billy Rowe's column—reading about the movie stars and other famous people made me feel good. I kept up with [actor] Herb Jeffries in those days. He was in the Theresa too." Herb Jeffries was the first black singing cowboy in the movies and starred in *Two Gun Man from Harlem* in 1938 and the western *The Bronze*

Buckaroo in 1939. He was a member of Duke Ellington's orchestra. KennerBelle Jackson's clippings included scoops from "Billy Rowe's Notebook" in the 1940s. She read the following: "Some of Harlem's hottest brown-skinned cuties have been haunting the avenue and the Theresa bar since word got out that the handsome crooning cowboy Herb Jeffries was in town and would be around on the Avenue—for a few weeks. . . . Pigmeat Markham didn't try to commit hari kari as the boys wanted people to believe, but left the gas on by mistake when he went to the land of not feeling no pains. . . . When the ugly custody fight between Noble and Ethel Sissle ended, she's got the kids back and they moved into the Hotel Theresa. Nobody knew the wherebouts of Noble. . . . The Cadillac dealers did big business in the 1940s. Seventh Avenue was overrun with them. . . . Taps Miller was driving a Cadillac in 1946. Both Taps and Charlie Carpenter were without visible means of support. Taps said the yodels were talking because he's got it and they don't know where he got it. A lot of residents would like to know what the secret was. . . . Milton Berle told a black audience a joke about Mayor O'Dwyer. Berle said he didn't show up because he was collecting numbers in Harlem. The sepia belt has been belted around enough without guys like Berle, who should know better than making dirty cracks about it in public spieling. In case he has missed the head-lines, all the figure gamblers are not in Harlem," Rowe admonished Berle, stating that the joke was in bad taste. ". . . One of the boys at Club Ebony has taken over Billie Holiday's heart and business affairs, however, hubby Jimmie Moore is talking to a lawyer. . . . Where, by the way, a few folks are wondering why Ralph Lampkins was sleeping in a car outside the Liberty since there was no room shortage. . . . However those who are looking for Charlie Glenn can find him at the Theresa refusing drinks after riding the wagon upward for two months. . . .

Eddie Rochester Anderson and Queen Maryed—in . . . from London . . . Oh, yes, just hang around, there's more!"

Dan Burley was another bard of the Hotel Theresa's 1940s heroic era. Together, "Burley and Rowe were Harlem's latter-day Damon Runyons," said the writer Tony Scherman. "Their cast of characters—the bandleaders, impresarios, showgirls, and wolves buzzing in and out of the Theresa's lobby—close kin to Runyon's guys and dolls, their Seventh Avenue and 125th Street a Times Square for readers who rarely went downtown."

A native of Chicago, Burley was a blues pianist who published a book on black slang called *Dan Burley's Original Handbook of Harlem Jive,* in 1944. During the 1940s, while serving as managing editor, he published a biweekly column with the *New York Amsterdam News* and contributed regularly to another Harlem weekly, the *New York Age.* "His stocky figure, gray-flecked head, and bulging eyes . . . familiar to patrons of the Savoy Ballroom and Hotel Theresa Bar," reads a January 1946 *Ebony* article. "[Burley] is eagerly read by the sporting uptown crowd, which he sometimes calls the 'nightlife backwash.' "

Burley's popular column was called "Back Door Stuff," and in its June 24, 1944, edition, subheaded "A Bolt Hit Harlem From the Heavy Blue," his all-seeing eyes were fixed on the Hotel Theresa: "The bolt of lightning that struck the Theresa on Monday morning was twenty-four to forty-eight hours too late. Saturday night, that bolt would have scared at least 789 into increasing the membership of local churches . . . all the playboys, hossplayers, the parlayers, the pick-up lads and the put-down men, the pigeon droppers and the lollypoppers, the stashers and the crashers who had the corner to themselves Saturday and Sunday night. Jack, that bolt of lightning would have emptied any bar and made many swear off forever, or else go down to the draft board and make a clean breast of it. It came too late. As it was, somebody said the lightning was hunting somebody up near the top floor. That lightning was after some cat who did something wrong!"

In the early 1940s a young man from Arkansas named John H. Johnson spent a number of months in the Hotel Theresa talking about starting a new magazine. He envisioned a pocket-size publication that would condense newspaper and magazine stories about black life. This idea turned out to be *Negro Digest,* which he began publishing in 1943. Two years later, Johnson started *Ebony,* and it was followed by *Jet* in 1951. The magazines published by the Johnson Publishing Company added even more luster to the already famous Hotel Theresa.

"Gee, it's great to wake up in Harlem," wrote Billy Rowe in the spring of 1946 as he focused on the happenings in the Theresa. "The whole town is talking about the *Ebony* spread on the Theresa." *Ebony*'s feature story on the Theresa with its array of photographs had black America talking. By this time there was no doubt that the hotel was "the social headquarters for Negro America, just as the Waldorf is the home for the white elite. To its registration desk flock the most famous Negroes in America. It is the temporary home of practically every outstanding Negro who comes to New York. It is common knowledge that Joe Louis stays there along with every big-time Negro fighter. So does Rochester and the Hollywood contingent, all the top bandleaders who haven't the good fortune to have their own apartments in town. Negro educators, colored writers, and the Liberian and Haitian diplomatic representative. Big men in the business world jostle top labor leaders in the flowered, mirrored lobby. . . . Today the hotel makes money with Negro business. The building and land are worth about one million dollars. Rooms are booked months in advance . . . and its rooms are always jammed." In the same article, *Ebony* reported that the child dancer Sugar Chile Robinson "stopped traffic with his dancing in the Theresa lobby."

"When Grace Nail Johnson, my husband, and I left the hotel to have dinner, we saw the midget and the others," recalled Jewel Sims Okala. "The same group of men were there nightly. When we were waiting for a car, we'd see other men walk up and talk with the regulars. It was like an 'old boys' meeting place. We thought they didn't work because they were like fixtures outside the hotel doors. We found humor in them. We'd laugh and say, 'They're still holding up the building.' That was our inside joke. Standing in front of buildings in those days was a pattern among certain black men. Of course, we never said anything to them, other than 'Good evening, gentlemen'—that sort of pleasantry. They were always very polite to us. There was a lot of gossiping in the Theresa. Grace, my husband, and I—we kept to ourselves. If you lived in the Theresa, there were certain people you really couldn't avoid."

Stories of celebrities in the Hotel Theresa reached blacks across America by print media and word of mouth. The hotel was also known as the international black headquarters. What gave the hotel its worldwide fame aside from the fact that the world's boxing champion, Joe Louis, made the hotel his New York residence? The Hotel Theresa was located in Manhattan, also the seat of the United Nations. Its physical proximity to the United Nations made it relatively easy for black activists in Harlem to connect with leaders of their fellow colonized Africans. In many ways, the struggle for African independence was brought to the stage on Seventh Avenue and 125th Street. Africans seeking independence saw the famous corner as a refuge to extol their cause, and as you will see, their cause ultimately became the cause of black America.

Four

THE QUEEN'S CORONATION

The only visible reminders that the white brick building at the corner of 125th Street and Seventh Avenue—now Adam Clayton Powell Jr. Boulevard—was once the famous Hotel Theresa are the dingy blue letters that still spell *Hotel Theresa* near the top of the building. It is the Theresa Towers building now, a business office, and just like the letters, the memories of the hotel it once was have faded in the minds of even those who were around to witness her story. Still, a few of Harlem's elderly occasionally stop as they pass the building and reminisce. The buoyancy, the courage, the aspirations, and the great capacity of the Harlemites for fun in those days make the hotel's heroic era a memorable time.

"I took some old friends by the Theresa not long ago. They had stayed there many times during the 1940s," recalled Harlem historian Preston Wilcox. "I asked the guards to let us in. They said, 'No, this ain't the Hotel Theresa no more. This is the Theresa Towers.' And I know those guys. They were acting all crazy. I kept telling them, 'You all know me. You been knowing me for years. I've been in this community since the 1950s.' The new owner of the building had made it plain that he didn't want anyone calling the building the Hotel Theresa, and he didn't want nobody who was remembering

Nat King Cole (*sitting*), Oscar Moore (*standing behind Nat King Cole*). *Photograph by John W. Mosley. Courtesy of the Charles L. Blockson Afro-American Collection, Temple University.*

the good old days trying to get inside. You see how things done changed uptown."

"Those old Theresa times were the best years of my life," said former Apollo Theater showgirl Naidine Collins. As she talked, her large, misty eyes betrayed a glitter reminiscent of the times when Harlem boogie-woogied all night. "The Theresa was where the action was—if you wanted to be in the know, if you wanted to be near the hip folks, you made your way to the Theresa. You could pass groups on the stoops, the curbside gangs, the drunks in bars, and all the joints in Harlem, and you still couldn't get the news or see the important people that you found when you got to the Theresa.

"If I could relive any time in the past, it would be those years. I came to the Theresa the first time in 1942. I was seventeen. In the Theresa's lobby, I left my new, expensive luggage at the desk while I went for a bellhop. My luggage was monogrammed with my initials, N.C. When I returned, there was a crowd around the desk. They thought Nat King Cole was checking in because we had the same initials. Can you believe that? I did go out with Nat a few times. He was a classy guy. But he dumped me because I wasn't putting out. Oh, I saw them all. Billy Eckstine. He had the sexiest voice—they called him 'the vibrato' in those days. There was Joe Louis. He and I were tight. But he never tried to hit on me; he was like my big brother. Joe didn't know if I was a man or a woman. When he was a greeter in Las Vegas in the seventies, I'd call him up and say, 'Joe, I'm coming out there.' When I got to Vegas, he'd take me on the town. And I never spent a dime.

"People in the Theresa used to confuse me with Dorothy Dandridge," Naidine added. "But to me, I looked better than her. I was lighter than Dorothy. She was the color I am now because I've gotten darker since those days. But do you know who I really looked like back then? I looked like Ava Gardner. I've got pictures when I was in my twenties, and I'm a dead ringer for her. My nose was straight like hers. With these added pounds, it's gotten wider." A few remember Naidine as a gorgeous woman with a stunningly exotic body who relished the whistles and winks she lured from guys on the make, particularly those who had money. "She was a dreamer. She was abused by a lot of men," recalled a former writer for the *Pittsburgh Courier*. "I know about her heartbreaks."

"Those old days are gone and they ain't never coming back," said Preston Wilcox. "The white man made us think that Harlem was worthless, and we bought his crap. Soon as they opened up downtown, we went running down there trying to be around white folk. Some of us would come back uptown bragging about being at the Waldorf or the Plaza. That's [the Hotel Theresa] where I spent my honeymoon in 1952. Lots of couples spent their honeymoon there because you could stay in a nice hotel and not have to pay to leave town. We don't know what we lost when we lost the Theresa. The old Harlem is gone and the Hotel Theresa went with it."

"The thought of losing Harlem didn't occur to us," said a businessman who runs a successful business downtown. "When the white hotels opened their doors and became friendlier, I wanted to do business there. We were stupid. We really didn't know any better. We told ourselves that all things white were better."

John Bennett Nail, an early Harlem businessman, answered the question about the lack of high-class, black-owned businesses in Harlem. He said black people who seek society, they cannot do it as whites with the same income. "There are no restaurants like Del-monico's or Sherry's for [black people]. There are not enough wealthy colored famiies to keep such a place going on the scale they would demand. So they do their entertaining at home. They spend more money on their home life, their dinners, and their parties than white men of the same income would, because they have no place to spend it outside."

"I remember being with Joe Louis, Jackie Robinson, and Billy Rowe in Frazier's," recalled Naidine Collins. "They were all talking about opening up a hotel. They talked for hours. But nothing was ever done about it. I remember them arguing over who would run the hotel. It seems to me that was a minor detail. It was a simple matter to me. They could have hired a person with a business back-ground to run the place. But they kept arguing about it. They were obviously not serious in the first place."

"When Southern blacks came to Harlem—those who had some money invested in Cadillacs and expensive clothes," said a Harlem businessman. "It was the West Indian black who invested in Harlem property."

Harlem hasn't always been home to black New Yorkers. It was mainly a white neighborhood until around 1900. Throughout its his-tory, Harlem experienced a long and arduous metamorphosis as it went from Dutch to Irish to Jewish to black. It was Harlem's final conversion that made it internationally famous as a black city located in the center of white Manhattan with more African-Americans to the square mile than any other place in the world.

Once blacks occupied Harlem, the ascendance of the Hotel Theresa as their cultural and intellectual headquarters was inevitable. Blacks have shown the ability to suck up life from the soil and create art and a gathering place in every Manhattan neighborhood they have inhabited. As they were permitted to move into new neighborhoods, they made an artistic and intellectual imprint time and time again, so that by the time the Hotel Theresa opened its doors to African-Americans, black talent and creativity were synonymous with Harlem.

By the time blacks made the Hotel Theresa their headquarters, they had been on Manhattan Island for over three hundred years. It all began when fifteen indentured African servants were brought to the Dutch settlement called New Amsterdam in 1610. The voyager Henry Hudson had been in search of a new route to Asia when he'd stumbled onto the island Native Americans called Manahatta. By 1664 the Dutch had surrendered to the English and New Amsterdam was renamed New York. The indentured servants became slaves. More slaves were imported to New York. The early slaves lived at the tip of Manhattan Island in the Bleecker and Canal Street areas.

Director-General Peter Stuyvesant had initiated a mandate to extend New York into Manhattan's northern reaches, an area replete with farmland and trees. The roads into this area were constructed by black slave labor. When the land was leveled, wealthy white entrepreneurs built mansions there and called the area Haarlem after a Dutch town.

A number of Africans slaves lived in Harlem. By 1709 a slave trading market was established on Wall Street. More slaves were brought into New York by the English. A number of their descendants lived and worked in the community. But the majority of Africans lived near the southern tip of Manhattan, where they stayed until 1827, when slavery was outlawed in New York. By 1830, the census reported that there were 13,976 blacks in Manhattan, and the majority were born in New York.

During these years, the New African Free School started by the Quakers gave black children an education while there existed no comparable institutions for white children. The African Free Schools were located on Mulberry near Grand Street.

Even at this time, we see blacks making appreciable inroads in the New York theater world. During this time, an article in *The New York National Advocate* reported the growing numbers of black productions in lower Manhattan. For the productions, these black thespians made a partition in the back of a house so that part of the space was used for dramatic plays. This space in a house near Mercer and Bleecker Streets was one of the earliest gathering places for blacks in the theater. In 1824, near Grove and Morton Streets, there was yet another house where dramatic plays were given by black performers at fifty cents for box seats and twenty-five cents for pit and gallery. These houses were gathering places for blacks especially on Monday nights.

Two years later on Spruce Street, the African Company performed representations of "Shakespeare's Proud Heroes." Elizabeth Taylor Green, known as the Black Swan, was a concert singer who performed with the African Company. In 1854, she traveled to England to perform at Buckingham Palace for Queen Victoria.

At the close of the Civil War, there were 15,000 Africans living in New York City. The majority of them were living in the areas of Lispenard, Broome, and Spring Streets. In these days, Washington Square Park was a bastion of wealthy life. Blacks who were in domestic service for white families were scattered in areas around the park. By 1880, a number of blacks were living on Sullivan, Thompson, Bleecker, Grove, and Minetta Lane, and nearby streets.

By the 1890s, a sizable concentration of the black population had migrated to the upper Twenties to the lower Forties west of Sixth Avenue. At the beginning of 1900, 4,982 blacks lived in San Juan Hill, while about three hundred fewer resided in Harlem. The largest concentration of blacks was in Brooklyn, which counted 18,367 black residents. Blacks made another shift in 1900 to the west Fifties and Sixties. Here, a new phenomenon sprang up on West Fifty-Third Street.

The Marshall and Maceo hotels were avant-garde centers for creative and intellectual black New Yorkers. The Maceo Hotel catered to a select clientele of clergy, educators, and businessmen. The Marshall Hotel, at 260 West Fifty-Third Street, was the vanguard for the Hotel Theresa. It was, in its day, the headquarters for black entertainers. Jimmie Marshall welcomed the most famous of the race, including vaudevillians, musicians, intellectuals, poets, and writers. There were always crowds of good-looking, well-dressed people in the Marshall, especially for the elegant Sunday dinners when guests dined on creole sauces and Maryland fried chicken while orchestra music played.

Composers James Reese Europe and Ford Dabney arrived at the Marshall from Washington, D.C., in 1900. They used the hotel as a musicians' training base to organize popular jazz bands. Europe and Dabney were among the early originators of popular jazz bands in New York. It remains unclear how long jazz bands had been traveling across the country, playing in honky-tonk dives and backwoods joints. But the first modern jazz band ever to appear on a New York stage, and likely any stage, was organized at the Marshall by Europe and Dabney. Their Clef Club Orchestra's first public appearance was at Harlem's Manhattan Casino in 1910.

The songwriters J. Rosamond Johnson and Bob Cole lived at the Marshall when they weren't touring the Continent. During the early 1900s, they were making a ton of money off their hit Broadway tunes "Under the Bamboo Tree" and "Since You Went Away." Paul Laurence Dunbar and Will Marion Cook collaborated to record "Clorindy, the Origin of the Cakewalk." Talents like Harry T. Burleigh, Abbie Mitchell, and Ada Overton were on the scene. Black composers were making their mark on American music, and white entertainers like Marie Cahill, Mae Irwin, and Theodore Drury couldn't resist reveling in the Marshall's limelight. Although Jim Crow was widespread, time and time again whites have followed blacks to their cultural centers on Manhattan Island.

The YMCA opened down the street from the Marshall and soon became an attraction for those interested in lectures, musicals, and vocational classes. A *Sun* newspaper reporter observed "The neighborhood is full of theatrical boarding houses . . . with their scandals, their romances, and their literary discussions. . . . In no other quarter of New York can there be found such elaboration of manners as in the boarding house parlors." Jimmie Marshall was an affable man who owned a couple of other brownstones, but the five-story Marshall Hotel was the grandest of his properties. After shows, tired and hungry performers could rouse Marshall no matter how late the hour, and the proprietor served them sandwiches and drinks.

In 1903, while the Marshall Hotel was in vogue, real estate entrepreneur Philip Payton planned an ingenious way to further invade white Harlem. He got help from an unlikely source. In addition to placing ads on the subway trains to advertise apartments in Harlem, he took advantage of an ongoing feud between two Jewish landlords on 134th Street. "To get even, one of them turned his house over to me to fill with colored tenants," said Payton. "I was successful in renting and managing this house, and after a time I was able to induce other landlords." That same year on Christmas Day, the *New York Herald Tribune* ran a story about the black invasion of Harlem: "Negroes Move Into Harlem . . . During the last three years the flats on 134th Street between Lenox and Seventh Avenues, that were occupied entirely by white folks, have been captured for occupancy by a Negro population. . . . The cause of the colored influx is inexplicable."

James Weldon Johnson recorded this account of how whites reacted to the threat of the black invasion of Harlem:

> In the eyes of the whites who were antagonistic, the whole movement took on the aspect of an "invasion"—an invasion of both their economic and their social rights. They felt that Negroes as neighbors not only lowered the values of their property, but also lowered their social status . . . their conduct could be compared to that of a community in the Middle Ages fleeing before an epidemic of the black plague . . . The presence of a single colored family in a block, regardless of the fact that they might be well-bred people, with sufficient means to buy their new home, was a signal for precipitate flight. The stampeded whites actually deserted house after house and block after block.

John E. Nail and Harry C. Parker opened a real estate office on 135th Street near Seventh Avenue around 1909. The partners purchased brownstones and tenements on 138th and 139th streets between Seventh and Eighth. The Nail and Parker Real Estate Company's business skyrocketed in 1911 through their purchases of nearly three blocks of tenements along 135th Street. A number of Harlemites have said that because John E. Nail was light enough to pass for white, this enabled him to buy much of the company's property from Jewish property owners. Ten blocks south, at Seventh Avenue and 125th Street, the hills were being leveled to make way for cigar manufacturer Gustav Seidenberg's new luxury hotel.

Seidenberg hired renowned architects Edward and George Blum to design a hotel to be located on Seventh Avenue and 125th Street. The Blum brothers were among the most talented architects of urban design during the first half of the twentieth century. Between 1910 and 1930, Edward and George Blum designed sixty-seven residential and office buildings in Manhattan. Seidenberg's hotel, completed in 1913, was a narrow, thirteen-story structure that displayed the Blums' distinctive use of light patterns of white terra-cotta ornament. Seidenberg named it in honor of his wife and originally intended it to be a whites-only establishment.

Isabel Jones, an early white resident of the Hotel Theresa, said, "Oh, it was a stylish place around 125th Street—lovely tall women and handsome men helping them in and out of their own private carriages, and everything was so green and quiet . . . I was a dressmaker then. I made them some lovely things, till my eyes gave out." She was interviewed in a 1946 issue of *Ebony* magazine. "All around Seventh Avenue were beautiful mansions."

Towering over its neighboring structures in the heart of Harlem's business district, the Hotel Theresa was accessible to the main lines of transportation accommodating New Jersey and Long Island in an era when 125th Street was an exclusive residential enclave and major business and cultural center in New York City. Seventh Avenue was an elegant center of entertainment filled with beautifully attired people. Years later, blacks added their particular pizzazz to the style on Seventh Avenue and 125th Street.

In the neighborhood were attractions like Oscar Hammerstein's Play House, advertised as "the finest in entertainment to the finest people in New York." The Harlem Opera House and Hartz and Seamon's Music Hall boasted such celebrities as Sophie Tucker and Fanny Brice. The New Orpheum Theater was another favorite playhouse. There were cinema theaters like Proctor's, the Victoria, and the Orient. Here, also, were banks, insurance companies, jewelry shops, bakeries, haberdashers. After a late night of entertainment, the wealthy clientele who dined at Pabst Restaurant often stayed overnight in the Hotel Theresa.

At the intersection of Seventh Avenue and 125th Street was a popular locale where stepladder suffragettes, socialists, and Communists declaimed their revolutionary speeches. For twenty-eight years, the hotel presided over this intersection admitting only white patrons.

By 1917, when the United States was at war, there was an increased influx of blacks from the South and areas in the Caribbean into certain areas of Harlem. Harlem was by no means characterized as a black area of town. African-Americans were scattered on various blocks extending from 130th to 140th streets and between Fifth and Seventh avenues in an area called the black belt. Whites occupied

130th Street down to 125th Street and below. Italians lived east of Fifth and as far south as Central Park North. The Irish and Jews occupied the areas west of Seventh Avenue. In those days, there was hostility between the black and Irish communities. The Irish had formed the infamous Canary Island Gang to keep non-Irish ethnic groups out of their neighborhood.

"There were always fights in those day," recalled former showgirl Ludie Jones. "The Irish kids didn't even want us to go into Central Park. I had to go through the park to get to school. And almost every day, I'd have to fight some Irish kid. There were Irish and black gangs so there was always street violence."

To the dismay of white Harlem, blacks began making substantial inroads into areas outside the black belt. Through the ingenuity of black real estate speculators who were aggressively purchasing Harlem properties, blacks from lower and mid-Manhattan and Brooklyn had invested in brownstones and tenements in unprecedented numbers by 1920. Businesswomen like Madam C. J. Walker and "Pigfoot" Mary were investing in Harlem real estate. Black churches, like the famed Abyssinian Baptist pastored by Adam Clayton Powell Sr., Mother African Methodist Episcopal, St. James Presbyterian, and Salem Methodist, followed the tidal wave uptown. A number of black political and social organizations like the NAACP and the Urban League opened branches in Harlem. Harlem became a choice place for what W. E. B. Du Bois had called the talented tenth—the professional, educated blacks who would pave the way for others to follow. A. Philip Randolph and Chandler Owen, who had started the *Messenger* magazine to promote a socialist movement, found offices in Harlem. Extolling a black nationalist philosophy, Marcus Garvey was in Harlem amassing one of the most influential international black movements in world history.

Despite efforts by whites to keep blacks cornered in restricted areas, masses of blacks were moving into the community. "A great migration," the playwright Wallace Thurman called it. "Southern Negroes, tired of moral and financial blue days, struck out . . . to seek adventure among factories, subways, and skyscrapers . . . New York to the Negro meant Harlem, and the great influx included not only thousands of Negroes from every state in the Union but also thirty thousand immigrants from the West Indian Islands and the Caribbean regions. Harlem was the promised land."

By the time masses of black actors, dramatists, intellectuals, journalists, and artists of note and distinction were arriving in Harlem, the Marshall Hotel had been closed nearly ten years. By now, the early civil rights movement was exploding based on the NAACP's court victories and gains by other civil rights groups. Blacks experienced a new self-confidence that spawned a greater degree of intellectual freedom. A new hope was abounding in the black community, and this hope gave birth to the Harlem Renaissance— the black literary movement of the 1920s that also ushered in the explosion of jazz. Vaudeville was a big part of entertainment. Dickie Wells, Eddie Rector, and Ralph Cooper danced in the variety shows across Harlem such as at the Lafayette Theater on Seventh Avenue and 131st Street and at the Lincoln Theater on Lenox Avenue and 135th Street. In 1921, the team of Eubie Blake and Noble Sissle presented the musical *Shuffle Along* on Broadway. Popular songs like "I'm Just Wild about Harry," "Gypsy Love Song," "Old Fashioned Love," and "Love Will Find a Way" came out of the musical.

Blacks were now closing in on areas near 125th Street, but not its business district, which included the Hotel Theresa. "When I moved to Harlem in 1930," said musician Alfred Cobbs, "there were lots of places along 125th Street we couldn't go in." Establishments farther uptown, such as the Cotton Club, were still barring blacks.

During the 1920s and 1930s whites came uptown to cavort in black nightclubs. The cultural renaissance and the explosion of jazz were Harlem phenomena that attracted worldwide attention. In those days Harlem's slumming parties were in vogue for whites as well. "There were two places they all wanted to see, Coney Island and Harlem," said Helen Lawrenson. "I took them to the usual tourist haunts: the Plantation and the Cotton Club; Clinton Moore's, a dimly lit apartment-club that catered to an epicenter coterie (titled male Britons flew there like homing pigeons almost the moment they hit New York) and which boasted a young black entertainer named Joey, who played piano and sang."

Bumpy Johnson made his contempt for the whites who came to Harlem after dark known to his white lover, Helen Lawrenson. "We ain't no zoo," he said. "How would you like it if we was to go downtown to your clubs and restaurants to stare at you people? Not that we'd get in. So why should we let you up here? I can't no way go downtown and walk into the Ritz. No way, no how. Except maybe I'm walkin' behind you, carryin' your bags, and then they'd get took away from me by some white bellboy because they wouldn't let me inside the door."

Harlem's nightlife was indeed something to remember. The 1920s and 1930s earned Harlem an international reputation as a place teeming with nightclubs, elegant ballrooms, theaters, and after-hour joints where movie stars flocked to hear big-name entertainers perform.

The Cotton Club, on Lenox Avenue and 142nd Street, has gone down in history as one of the top entertainment spots in the world. It had moved downtown by the time the Theresa was integrated, but the Cotton Club helped to put Harlem on the map, and it shows why the ambience of Harlem was critical to the success of nightspots of the era. Arguably, it was the hippest nightclub in the world during the 1920s and 1930s. The club attracted people from every station in life and from all over the world. Originally called Jack Johnson's Club, it was founded by the black heavyweight boxing champion in the teens. But white gangsters George "Big Frenchy" DeMauge and Owney Madden easily forced Johnson out of his club. As powerful mobsters, they had lucrative businesses in the rackets, including money laundering, bootlegging, murder, and speakeasies. The club permitted only white patrons. It made exceptions for a few blacks like Joe Louis and the actress Fredi Washington, who had appeared in the movie *Imitation of Life.* Partygoers jumped to the beat of music by Duke Ellington, Lucky Millinder, the Mills Blue Rhythm, and Jimmie Lunceford. Add that bevy of "high yaller" chorus girls like Billie Cain, Lillian Powell, the Moses sisters, Elida Webb, and Dot Rhodes to that huge stockpile of talent because they were something for white men to look at. Seeking more fame and fortune, the Cotton Club left Harlem in 1936 and moved to Broadway. Even with all its glory and with all the money on Broadway, it lost its beat and died downtown with the white folks. Something about the club's being in Harlem had made it jump.

There was Mike's place competing with the Cotton Club for

customers. The all-night spot was on Seventh Avenue and 143rd Street. You had to be there when the sun shone to recognize all the famous white people who were slumming in Harlem. Mike's was like a sensational out-of body experience where bathtub gin flowed till dawn; these were the days of Prohibition. Partygoers breathed its air all night and came up with bizarre tales that soon hit Harlem's streets. Big-time showbiz orchestra leaders like the Duke, Erskine Hawkins, and Buddy Johnson had the very rich, the near rich, and the not-so-rich boogying to jazz and blues tunes like "Hard Hearted Hannah," "Fascinatin' Rhythm," and "Lovin' Sam."

The Savoy Ballroom, the block-long dance hall on Lenox Avenue and 141st Street was opened in 1926 by white luggage maker and talent agent Moe Gale. The Savoy Ballroom welcomed a racially diverse group. It was so radically mixed and so inclusive that its clientele hasn't been duplicated anywhere since. The ballroom was the first place where interracial couples were seen dancing together without incident. The sizzling jazzy sounds of Louis Armstrong, Coleman Hawkins, Chick Webb, Harry Carney, Joe Nanton, Roy Eldridge, and Duke Ellington were transmitted by radio across the world, which made the Savoy universally famous.

Off the main strip, twenty-five-cent parlor parties brought in the customers. At these parties in brownstones and apartments, the furniture was moved out of the parlor where the dancing took place. The variety of soul food was in the dining room. Choices of entertainment were available. There were poker games and liquor for sale. Live music with risqué lyrics and exotic dancing were part of the action. "Men walking along the street would hear music and go up several flights of stairs—usually every other floor was without lights after ten or eleven p.m.—pay his twenty-five cents, go in, and often have a ball with complete strangers," said musician Walter Thomas.

The Nest Club on 133rd Street and Seventh stayed open all night if the customers behaved. Among some of the better known spots were the Club Alabam east of Lenox on 129th Street, the Sugar Cane on Fifth Avenue and 134th Street, and Leroy's at 135th and Fifth Avenue. Long after the rest of New York had gone to sleep, the Chicken Shack, Dickie Wells, and Jenny Lou's served up soul food to the night owls, so good, as the old-timers would say, that it could make you "slap your mama."

During the 1930s, long lines of limousines from Park and Fifth avenues were parked outside Harlem's smoky lairs. When the popular clubs closed in the wee hours of the morning, a number of partygoers hunted the neighborhood for its reputed clandestine speakeasies and notorious houses to satisfy outlandish pleasures. The racy action in these hideouts lasted until seven or eight most mornings. Still, Harlem provided a high-toned nightlife that made it the hippest shindig in America.

All the while, blacks who waited for the Seventh Avenue bus outside the Hotel Theresa in the evenings could only peer through the venetian blinds and fantasize about being part of such a luxurious place where elegantly dressed whites met at the bar and mingled in the lobby after an evening of entertainment on 125th Street. Blacks heard sounds of gaiety and laughter. Sissle and Blake's tunes flowed from the Theresa bar. Still, blacks were barred—a nightly reminder of white privilege.

Artists of the Harlem Renaissance gazed in awe at the elegant structure that was the Hotel Theresa. Its grand ballroom on the hotel's top floor was mysteriously locked. Harlem writers envisioned each of its four hundred seats occupied by Harlem's talented group of artists. In fact, a number of writers of the era proposed to the hotel's managers that it be made into a gathering place for black artists and intellectuals so they could have a lovely, tranquil setting similar to places downtown that discriminated. This proposal clashed with the hotel's whites-only policy in the days when white New Yorkers referred to it as "the hotel uptown." "I remember when no blacks worked there [the Theresa]," said the bandleader Andy Kirk. "That was in the early days."

There were no clean, respectable hotels for blacks in Harlem in the 1930s. A number of musicians reluctantly stayed at Love B. Woods's Woodside Hotel on Lenox Avenue and 147th Street, despite its unsavory reputation. "The Woodside Hotel was the black hotel. That is where some of us went if we came to New York for a short stay," Andy Kirk said.

The hit song "Jumping at the Woodside," by Cab Calloway, made the hotel a popular hangout for musicians and the fast crowd.

"Woods owned a few other hotels in Harlem," recalled the writer James Booker. "He ran a bunch of dingy flophouses, so he didn't attract the more refined elements of the race. There was money in flophouses with its clientele of pimps and prostitutes, and gangsters. Love B. Woods was used to making his money that way. He didn't know how to run a classy place. He only knew how to be an innkeeper to hoodlums—that ilk."

In 1936, Woods's corporation made an offer to the Seidenberg family to purchase the Theresa Hotel. Woods dreamed of transforming the Theresa into the black Waldorf-Astoria of Harlem, but his bid fell short. He believed that the Seidenberg family set the price too high. Still, there was no comfortable hotel for refined dark-skinned visitors to New York.

The Great Depression ravaged Harlem and silenced many of its creative voices. Tuberculosis and too much gin cut Wallace Thurman's life short in 1924. James Weldon Johnson died in 1938. Nella Larsen, author of *Passing* and *Quicksand,* moved to Brooklyn and lived in a mysterious, obscure manner. The legendary Zora Neale Hurston returned to her native Florida and lived like a semirecluse. Poet Jean Toomer immersed himself in religious mysticism. And Jessie Fauset, Charles S. Johnson, Countee Cullen, and Arna Bontemps devoted themselves fully to teaching. Of the Harlem Renaissance writers, only Langston Hughes remained visible after the 1930s ended.

The economic drought deeply affected Harlem's nightlife, leaving it almost barren for nearly a decade. Only Smalls' Paradise and Elk's Rendezvous continued operating throughout the lean years. Big-name entertainers were nowhere to be seen uptown. Dickie Wells was gone and all those other little cellar dives where all-night fun could be had. Now, the hottest night scene in New York was downtown. Broadway became the new center for blacks performing for white audiences. The Palace, Loews State, the Capitol, the Roxy, the Zanzibar, and the New Amsterdam now showcased a variety of black talent like Bill "Bojangles" Robinson, Ethel Waters, Duke Ellington, and Ella Fitzgerald.

Harlem had faded to black by now. White patronage no longer

existed. The Theresa was in a black neighborhood now, and the loss of white patronage meant the hotel's survival was at stake. So, the Theresa's management announced a change. On a windy March day in 1940, an official of the Gresham Management Company placed the keys to the newly renovated Hotel Theresa in the hands of a new manager, Walter W. Scott. This change in management symbolized the major shift in the dynamics of Harlem, for Scott, a YMCA executive, was black.

African-Americans, who could now patronize the hotel, saw this as evidence of what they could achieve if given the opportunity. The announcement of the new policy was made in the *New York Age*. It read: "Harlem Hotel Seeks Negro Trade; Picks Manager: The Hotel Theresa at Seventh Avenue and 125th Street, which catered to white patronage for several years, has changed its policy as of March 20 and will cater to both races, under Negro management with a Negro staff, according to an announcement by Richard Thomas, publicity manager of the hotel. In carrying out its new policy for the accommodation of Negroes and whites, the Gresham Management Company, operators of the Theresa, appointed Walter Scott as the hotel's manager. Extensive renovations and improvements of the services and facilities of the hotel have been undertaken. A staff of 80 persons has been employed."

Walter W. Scott was a bellhop, porter, and waiter on the Hudson River Day Line boats. A graduate of New York University and a World War I veteran, he was a business manager at Harlem's 135th Street YMCA. In early April, Walter and Gertrude Scott and their sixteen-year-old daughter, Gladys, moved into a spacious six-room suite on the tenth floor.

"Gertrude Scott was a professional seamstress," recalled Jewel

Sims Okala. "She and her daughter weren't visible around the hotel. Gertrude Scott was from the old school, which meant it wasn't proper for ladies to be seen in certain areas of the hotel. Places like the bar were out of the question for refined ladies. Young Gladys was a psychology major at New York University."

The year that the hotel welcomed blacks, there were achievements on a few other fronts for blacks in Harlem. Richard Wright's landmark novel, *Native Son,* was a runaway best seller. After moving into the Hotel Theresa, Sugar Ray Robinson made his professional boxing debut. And the 135th Street library was named for Arthur Alfonso Schomburg, who had died two years before.

Few African-Americans had stayed in the Theresa prior to Scott's ascendancy as manager in 1940, boxing champion Joe Louis and Lena Horne among them.

"We've got the top hotel in Harlem here," said Walter Scott. "Bellboys, room service, cleaning and pressing, phones in the rooms, a beauty parlor, a restaurant, and a bar right in the building." As manager, Walter Scott made sure advertisements on the black hotel appeared in the major black newspapers across the nation. An ad in the *Pittsburgh Courier* read, "The Testimony of Thousands: It's the Hotel Theresa when in New York any season of the year. Seventh Avenue and 125th Street . . . in the heart of Harlem . . . 300 spacious rooms; all outside rooms; luxurious suites, orchid room for dining; cocktail lounge and bar; the lovely mezzanine for relaxation; ideal atmosphere for rest, study, and comfort."

"Walter Scott was pure class," recalled former barmaid Ruth Guzzman. "He was golden brown and tall—good-looking and very distinguished. I was young and I thought he was serious all the time.

But now I know he was trying to put forth a good image for the hotel."

Isabel Jones, the white resident who was interviewed in *Ebony*, was asked what the transition under Walter Scott was like. "I like it here fine. The women on my floor are real pleasant to me, and though they say the hotel has gotten pretty noisy and wild lately, I never hear any of it. I'm way up here and the manager lives on my floor, so nobody dares make any noise or they'd get thrown out.

"There were fifteen whites living in the hotel when it was integrated. My, when the colored people took over, I was so frightened! I thought they'd make me go away, that they'd want their hotel all for themselves. But mercy, they've been so kind. They let me stay on, and what's more, I don't have to pay as much as the other guests because I was here long before any of 'em when it didn't cost so much to live here.

"Of course, when I have to go out for something to eat, the colored people aren't so nice—they have regular days when they push all the whites on the sidewalks, and I've gotten more than my share of shoves. The first colored people moved into the neighborhood about twenty-five years ago—then more and more came, till finally it got like you see it now—all colored. There were some colored folk living in the hotel for some time before Mr. Scott came in 1940, and for about three years afterward there were lots of whites here.

"But now all but about fifteen of them have died or moved away. Me—I'm not going to die here, believe me? I've been waiting for my boyfriend to come back for too many years—I'm going to find me a man with money and marry him. I could make a man happy—I make fine cookies. Just look at this recipe book," Jones said, holding it up.

"And if that doesn't work, I'll go to Hollywood. When I take my teeth out, I look just like a witch."

"One of the first things Scott did as manager was to move Big Steve," recalled tap dancer Leroy Meyers. "Back before the hotel let blacks in, there was only one black bartender. His name was Big Steve. He was a big, burly, dark-skinned man. There was a joke around Harlem that Walter Scott put Big Steve in the window so that black people would know that it was all right to come to the hotel. Steve had never worked in the window till Walter Scott put him there."

Not since the days of the old Marshall Hotel had there been a place as nice as the Theresa where black people could gather. "I thought it was such a class hotel when it was integrated," recalled musician Joe Wilder. "We had nothing as nice in the neighborhood."

Five

CELEBRITIES AND NIGHTLIFE

Within walking distance of some of the world's most famous entertainment, the Theresa was the axis for Harlem's nightspots where the hot sounds of jazz with risqué lyrics and exotic dancing lasted till dawn. In the early 1940s, the King Cole Trio, Lucky Millinder, Billy Eckstine, Jimmie Lunceford, and the Ink Spots were living in the Hotel Theresa.

Among the first actors that Scott welcomed to the Theresa were the cast of *The Notorious Elinor Lee,* which opened the year the hotel was integrated. *Elinor Lee* was the last film produced under the banner of the Oscar Micheaux Film Corporation. It featured Robert Earl Jones and Edna Mae Harris. The comic, actor, and all-around entertainer Eddie Green, who was also in the film, loved living in the hotel and made it his full-time residence. He starred in *Dress Rehearsal,* which was the first all-black film made for television, shown on NBC in New York City in 1940. In 1943, Lena Horne, Rex Ingram, and Ethel Waters, fresh from the movie set of *Cabin in the Sky,* were staying in the Theresa.

Billy Rowe focused on his friend Lena Horne in a 1944 column when he sarcastically wrote, "All this national radio stuff about Lena Horne being wedded to a white man of music is being denied in

Nat King Cole plays as audience looks on, 1940s. *Photograph by John W. Mosley. Courtesy of the Charles L. Blockson Afro-American Collection, Temple University.*

so-called in-the-know-circles. Horne herself told the *Notebook* that it ain't so, but how are we to know?"

The Cinderella story of the Ink Spots is legendary. In 1936, four young men were working as porters in the basement of the Paramount Theater in New York City. One afternoon the famous talent agent Moe Gale was in the building attending a business meeting. As he was leaving from a side exit, a rich blend of voices wafted upstairs, singing:

> *Dinah,*
> *Is there anyone finah*
> *In the state of Carolinah . . .*

"There was one voice that stood out," recalled Gale. "A high, almost feminine tenor." Startled and delighted, Gale raced down to the basement, where he found four black men. They looked at Gale, threw their eyes back to the floor, and nervously began sweeping. Gale asked them who was singing. Fearing they would lose their $12-per-week jobs, they said, "Nossir, we weren't singing." The small white man realized their fear and insisted that they sing for him. Deek Watson, Hoppy Jones, Charlie Fuqua, and Billy Kenny sang for Moe Gale. Four years later, the young men called themselves the Ink Spots. Gale moved them into the Theresa Hotel. Their hit song "If I Didn't Care" was an international sensation. In 1940, Moe Gale had the group booked into the same Paramount Theater where he'd discovered them. They were now earning $2,500 a week and styling and profiling on Seventh Avenue in their new Cadillacs. A few years later, Billy Rowe wrote about the success of the group:

Dizzy Gillespie (*left*), and Leonard Feather, 1940s. *Photograph by John W. Mosley. Courtesy of the Charles L. Blockson Afro-American Collection, Temple University.*

"The Ink Spots made a sensational invasion of Europe, and officials of the Bank of England sat right down and cried because they were getting that much dough."

There were nearly a hundred well-known black orchestras in New York at the time. People from other cities thought of Harlem as a place where the nightclubs, filled with celebrities, jumped all night. As the entertainers began enjoying life in the Hotel Theresa, Harlem's nightlife began to explode by the mid-1940s. Harlem's nightlife was exhilarating and tantalizing—throbbing to the beat of hot jazz and urbane in its unusual sophistications and rich with international lure—Harlem was unforgettable to all who came, and the Hotel Theresa was at the center of it all because the performers were calling the hotel home.

Another reason Harlem's nightlife skyrocketed was that club owners shifted their long-standing policies and decided to hire "big name" performers to compete with Broadway; Billy Rowe offered the owners some sound advice: "The promoter must take cognizance of the fact that the days are past when you can buy a band and just throw your doors open to the public and be guaranteed a full house." Now the owner had to advertise heavily, work hard, and use every ingenious method available to bring in the crowds. Billy Rowe said that theaters and nightclubs in Harlem would do better if they put showmanship back into show business instead of trying to cut the salaries of acts when even the sky was no limit where living costs were concerned.

By 1945, when the Theresa was at its pinnacle of fame, half a dozen nightspots uptown were competing for black business. African-Americans entertainers who performed uptown relished the idea of staying at the Theresa. Great songs were fashioned in those days, and a number of them were written in the Theresa Hotel. The King Cole Trio wrote such hit tunes as "Sweet Lorraine," "Honey Suckle Rose," and "Hit That Jive." "The manner in which Nat King Cole softly sings 'Nature Boy' has got Broadway all ears," said Billy Rowe. "However, Harlem goes strong for the flipover."

Bands were formed, musicians jammed, and musicians were booked in the hotel. "Buck Clayton used to send for me to come up to his room at the Theresa. I used to deliver copies of his music to his band members," said Horace Carter.

Songwriter Dallas Bartley lived in the Theresa Hotel between 1943 and 1947. Known for "Early in the Morning," a hit song that he cowrote with Louis Jordan and Leon Hickman, Bartley composed some of his music on hotel napkins.

The Club Baron, Jock's Place, and Club Sudan were among Harlem's hippest nightspots. The Club Sudan, operated in the old Cotton Club, grabbed headlines by having its opening gala on Thanksgiving night and hiring topflight entertainers like Billy Eckstine, whose hits songs "Caravan," "Prisoner of Love," and "You Go to My Head" brought down the house. Those who packed in on the gala nights were thrilled by the bands and the floor shows, which included tap dancing and a chorus line. "Canfield and Lewis, the show-stoppers at the Sudan Club, were the funniest comedy duo to hit Harlem niteries in many moon," said Billy Rowe. Frank Lazama, manager of the Sudan, filled up the place by hiring such greats as Count Basie and Illinois Jacquet. In a 1946 column, Billy Rowe said they would be aired over WLIB radio.

The old Elk's Rendezvous had revitalized its shows and was making an effort to compete with the group of new nightclubs. It hired its share of high-priced superstars like headliners Peg Leg Bates and Savannah Churchill. The chorus girls, now all unionized and well-paid, were showstoppers.

During the 1920s and 1930s, blacks couldn't afford Harlem's nightlife. Now the niteries were overflowing with black and white patrons.

The Club Baron, on 132nd and Lenox, was the most sophisticated and luxurious of the black clubs in the nation. "I owed my many friends something in return for their patronage," said owner John Barone. He built a nightclub "that would offer every, if not more, pleasure than one finds in a Broadway club." Barone offered top salaries to entertainers that matched those paid by downtown club owners. Rising star Larry Steele was the master of ceremonies at the Club Baron. Barone hired Hortense "the Body" Allen to take charge of his bevy of beautiful leggy chorus girls. He looked to the big-name field and hired Ivy Anderson, the former singer for Duke Ellington, and Ethel Waters to pack the house. Ethel Waters was receiving $2,000 per week. No other entertainer in a Harlem nightclub had been paid so high a salary.

If you stood outside the Theresa on 125th Street in the 1940s, the glittering marquee of the Apollo Theater could be seen. Located between Seventh and Eighth avenues on 125th Street, the Apollo Theater had the rare distinction of having never barred admission to blacks. Opened in 1935 by Frank Schiffman and Leo Brecher, the four-story building was originally constructed for the old Hurtig Seamon burlesque theater in 1904.

Count Basie playing the piano, 1940s. *Photograph by John W. Mosley. Courtesy of the Charles L. Blockson Afro-American Collection, Temple University.*

Before the Apollo, Frank Schiffman managed the Layfayette Theater. In this theater were the Lafayette players, Harlem's first black acting troupe. Among the Lafayette players were actors like Frank Wilson, Charles S. Gilpin, Percy Verwayne, Abbie Mitchell, Edna Thomas, and Lenore Ulric.

The Apollo is one of the rare jewels in American cultural history. Any black performer of jazz, dance, all-around entertainer, or anyone whose been in an Apollo audience understands the uniqueness of the theater. No one appreciated this more than the tap dancer Honi Coles who said, "As far as I'm concerned, the black show business that I know had its orgins in the Apollo. All the great, great, great performers who really were the beginning even of the Apollo and the Lafayette are dead. Like the Chick Webbs, the Bert Williamses, and other performers of the teens and twenties—they're all gone, and a whole new type of show business sprang up with the ascendancy of the Apollo." People who went to the Apollo Theater in the 1930s and 1940s dressed up for the occasion—the women in high heel shoes, hats, and gloves. The men were appropriately groomed in suits and ties.

A performer could appear at the Earle in Philadelphia, the Howard in Washington, or the Regal in Chicago, but black entertainers had not suceeded in the big league until they played the Apollo. This was the case until the 1960s.

The biggest names in jazz and rhythm and blues, such as Count Basie, Cab Calloway, Ella Fitzgerald, Lena Horne, Paul Williams, Nat King Cole, Billy Eckstine, Fats Navarro, Arthur Prysock, Ray Charles, and Dinah Washington, established their national reputations at the Apollo while living in the Theresa Hotel.

"Back in those days, after guys like Billy Eckstine, Arthur Prysock, and Cab Calloway became famous, they would return to play the Apollo," said trumpet player Danny Moore. "You don't see that happening with the greats today. They think its beneath them to return to the Apollo."

"When a young kid from Tennessee named Elvis Presley made his first trip to New York, he went straight to the Apollo Theater," said Harlem disc jockey Hal Jackson. "He saw [Theresa Hotel resident] Bo Diddley drive the audience crazy with his hip-gyrating performance. Buddy Holly, another young white performer out of Texas, incorporated Diddley's double-rhythm guitar pattern into his playing."

Harlem had indeed recaptured the title of capital of nightclub entertainment. By 1945 whites were streaming into Harlem again to party, listening to jazz and enjoying the great floor shows. Not since the old days of the Cotton Club and the Savoy had Harlem been studded with nightclubs, after-hours spots, and late-night food joints.

The Palm was a combination club and restaurant, across the street from the Hotel Theresa. It was a hangout for Sidney Poitier and Harry Belafonte when they were emerging on the showbiz scene. Jazz artists like Billy Eckstine, Buck Clayton, and Duke Ellington were regulars in the Palm. Politicians like Adam Clayton Powell Jr. and Hulan Jack often dropped in. "One night I was in the Palm," remembered Danny Moore. "There was the world's greatest vocalist, Billy Eckstine, arguing with Titus Turner. Titus wrote the lyrics to 'Fever.' I was a bit surprised because Billy was arguing that he sung better than some other singer. Billy didn't have to stoop to that level. He was one of the greatest singers of all time. Billy could get good and rowdy. He didn't take no shit. I put it to you this way, he wasn't to be messed with. He called himself the Fabian of the 1940s. I say if you got it, flaunt it. He had it. He had the hottest—with hit songs like 'Caravan' and 'You Go to My Head.' "

Popular radio personality Phil Gordon hosted a late-night radio

Duke Ellington playing the piano, 1940s. *Photograph by John W. Mosley.*
Courtesy of the Charles L. Blockson Afro-American Collection, Temple University.

show that was aired from the Palm. The famous radio program aired in two parts. *The 1280 Club* was one program, and *Life Begins at Midnight* was the other. When Duke Ellington, Lena Horne, Ella Fitzgerald, or Illinois Jacquet stopped by the Palm, they'd usually be interviewed for one of the radio programs.

There was the hot jazz house Minton's, in the Cecil Hotel, where Thelonious Monk, Charlie Parker, and Dizzy Gillespie gave birth to bebop. "Members of my band and others always went to Minton's to jam," said Andy Kirk. "That is where they really got the feeling of what the others were doing, style. That kind of thing happened in Kansas City."

Comedian Nipsey Russell, "Harlem's son of fun," and his famous torch singers made the Baby Grand an in-spot. Located at 319 West 125th Street, the Baby Grand Café served Chinese-American seafood, choice of wines and liquors, steaks, chops, and the house specialty, Southern fried chicken.

Smalls' Paradise, the oldest nightclub in Harlem, had the best tap dancers of all the nightspots. Ed Smalls, owner of Smalls' Paradise, was a known hustler who ran a gambling operation in one of his back rooms. "Wondah what did Ed Smalls mean when he had his pretty eye-catching secretary call to tell us that 'Po' Slim Hall, working away down there in the Nation's Capital, had sent along ten bucks to aid the Jackie Robinson Day of last Tuesday," said Billy Rowe. "The little man of the Paradise collected more than eight hundred bucks himself . . . the Mirror charged him with ticket scalping for the all important day." Tap dancer Leroy Meyers said, "Everybody in Harlem knew that Ed Smalls was a bagman."

There was an after-hours, clandestine spot on 148th and St.

Nicholas Avenue. It was run by Chink Cunningham and Johnny Walker. The building was a nondescript brownstone without a sign. Those in the know understood that it was a numbers and bookmaking place. Cunningham and Walker admitted a select clientele like Joe Louis, Lana Turner, Billy Daniels, Billy Eckstine, Romare Bearden, and Tallulah Bankhead, who loved to gulp down bourbon. "I saw Tallulah Bankhead drink bourbon," recalled Evelyn Cunningham. "She did drink lots of it."

Six

BACK DOOR STUFF (1940–48)

W hen my parents came to visit me from Ohio in the 1940s," said Harlemite Terry Layne, "I put them in a lovely suite in the Theresa Hotel. After they unpacked and seemed to be comfortable in their surroundings, they asked me to take them to Harlem."

"The Hotel Theresa was one of the showcases of the community," said trumpet player Joe Wilder. "The only one on that level. There is no place today of that status."

Although the hotel's character and appearance were significant, it was the action that occurred within its walls that was most compelling. In other words, the amenities offered by the hotel were secondary to the star-studded guests who stayed under its roof. Today, every former patron has his or her own story of the Hotel Theresa— stories that take us through corridors, behind the doors of suites, into corners of the bar and public meeting places, out onto the streets, and into the very life of Harlem.

If two or more Harlemites of the Theresa's heroic era get together, they will surely reminisce about life in the hotel and the days when Harlem was the Mecca of nightlife.

"There were so many people night and day beneath the marquee, most from out of town," recalled *Pittsburgh Courier* writer

Evelyn Cunningham. "These were sporting types who went across the country to follow big events. I was so amused to watch men from out of town swinging their golf clubs or wearing a riding habit because they thought this was the thing to do in New York. They thought you've got to pretend to be a golfer or an equestrian. Therefore you arrive in a car, the doorman takes out your golf bag. You are at the world-famous Hotel Theresa. So you stand outside and let everybody see you. I could see them from my window in the *Courier* offices across the street from the hotel. Some of them would stand outside the Theresa all day, strolling back and forth. It used to tickle me to death.

"I was looking out of the my window at the *Courier* one day and I recognized a man I knew from Pittsburgh. He was standing in front of the hotel dressed in golf clothes and carrying his golf clubs while strolling up and down Seventh Avenue. I knew this man, and he didn't know one thing about the game of golf. I knew that he'd heard all the myths and stories about the Theresa. He thought he needed to bring his golf clubs to look impressive."

Former barmaid Ruth Guzzman, who insisted on being called a mixocologist, had a more romanticized opinion of the out-of-towners. "When those good-looking black men came to town from Detroit and Chicago following Joe Louis and checked into the hotel, they would have their golf clubs, and I knew they had money," recalled Guzzman. "There weren't many black men swinging golf clubs who had money in the early 1940s. They were rich and fabulous black men. I knew a lot of women who got in on that action. A barmaid is a whiskey pourer. I was a mixocologist. That takes training."

"I'd walk up and down Seventh Avenue in my riding boots—

wearing the whole riding outfit just to be seen," recalled former showgirl Betty Stanton. "It was important for me to look like I had money in those day so that somebody else who had money would want to take me out. My image was important. I got a whole lot of attention in that riding habit from black and white men. The riding habit was the in thing to wear around the hotel. I usually wore it on Saturdays and Sundays. There were a lot of us walking along Seventh Avenue in riding clothes. I wasn't the only one. Looking back, it was important to me to look like somebody. I had no education. I wanted to be a nurse. Harlem Hospital had a nursing program but I couldn't afford to go there." (It was well known in Harlem circles that Marva Louis, Joe's wife, was an accomplished equestrian. A number of wannabes, especially women, may have been imitating her.)

"The grandiose behavior exhibited by some in the hotel who wore riding and golf clothes revealed a lack of self-acceptance," said clinical psychologist Paula Owens. "Usually they are trying to fool others and themselves."

The double doors beneath the marquee opened to a wide foyer that revealed a lighted lobby. When visitors walked in, they were struck by the glistening mirrors and green and beige floral paper that covered the high walls. Freshly polished white, square tiles with black stripes covered the entire first floor. Eloise Scott, a slender, golden brown lady with a friendly face, stood behind the registration desk to greet visitors. Always smiling, Eloise Scott was continually shifting the heavy registration book back and forth for guests to sign in. A set of elevators was adjacent to the registration desk. Three public telephone booths were next to the elevator. While waiting to register, a number of guests greeted old friends, waited for dates, and looked for celebrities who were usually on the scene.

The writer Albert Murray spent his honeymoon in the hotel in 1942. He recalled, "There were always crowds in the lobby, night and day. It was scintillating. Bunch of good-looking, successful, famous people. Who was more hip than the guys in Harlem or better looking than the gals?"

Longtime Harlemite Mary Louise Williams noted that the hotel was a magnet for European and other foreign white women who wanted black men. The Theresa was certainly internationally known by the mid-1940s because of Joe Louis's world-wide fame. And by now, everybody knew that he called the Hotel Theresa home whenever he was in New York. White women from the Continent traveled to New York to the Theresa to meet black men. The black men they picked up were referred to as players. These white women knew that the best-looking black men would be in the Theresa, and they would be easy to attract. It seemed to be a strong attraction: white women wanted black men and black men wanted white women. "Yes, there were prostitutes of both races in the hotel," recalled Mary Louise Williams. "That's no different from white exclusive hotels in downtown New York. So prostitutes were in the Theresa because powerful men were there, and prostitutes follow powerful men."

"I could always spot the white Communist women in the lobby," recalled Evelyn Cunningham. "They were sent to the Theresa to seduce black men. The Theresa was one of their recruitment centers because so many black men were always in the hotel. There was no other place in Harlem where so many black men were in one place. No, I don't remember the Communist women being in the bar. They may have gone into the coffee shop. But it was really the lobby where I saw them. They wore old, tattered clothes. Black women in the hotel wouldn't have been caught dead in those old clothes. After a white woman came into the lobby to pick her mark, an hour or so later I'd see some poor fellow walking out with her. Black women didn't want to join the party because we weren't going to dress like Communist women. Most of the black men in the party were married to white women. Black women had very little power in the party."

The Harlem Communist Party had a strong membership, especially among black men. Racism and the low economic fortunes of Harlemites caused a number of blacks to join.

"My husband was Julius Okala. He was a colleague of Eslanda Robeson, Benjamin Davis, and John Henrik Clarke," said hotel resident Jewel Sims Okala. "They were on panels together at the Theresa, Columbia University, or sometimes the 135th Street library. Julius was enthusiastic about attending lectures and giving speeches—he was an intellectual and he enjoyed these events. [Giving a speech titled "Africa and World Peace," in 1946, Julius Okala said, "If you hurt a child, he has several ways of getting back at you when he grows up." He added that unless the people of Africa were given a part in world government, they would be forced to use their acquired knowledge and power against their oppressors.] The U.S. government was keeping tabs on a lot of people in the hotel in those days, including my husband. The Theresa was where important black people stayed when they visited New York. When Mary McLeod Bethune came to New York to give a series of lectures at Columbia University, she stayed at the Theresa Hotel. She was always dressed beautifully. Benjamin Mays was there. I'd see him in the elevator occasionally. Those of us in the hotel understood that the FBI was around."

"Every year the Communist Party USA held its national convention there," said the writer Stephen Holmes, "bringing with it delegates and a number of white men in suits sitting in cars outside the hotel, taking pictures of everyone coming and going."

When the Harlem Communist Party leader Benjamin Davis ran for the New York City Council in 1943 and 1945, he was supported by such celebrities as Lena Horne, Ella Fitzgerald, Count Basie, Coleman Hawkins, and the gangster Bumpy Johnson. Charlie Parker performed benefits for his campaigns. (Benjamin Davis Jr. served as New York City councilman from Harlem from 1943 to 1947.)

"Many men joined the party for jobs, not for political reasons," said Judge James Watson. "Nobody in Harlem cared that they were working for Communists. They wanted to make a living—put food on the table. It wasn't about ideology."

According to the writer Stephen Holmes, in 1940, only 12 percent of African-Americans between the ages of twenty-five and twenty-nine had finished high school. Only 2 percent had finished college. Less than 2 percent of professionals were black males. Less than 3 percent of doctors were black. And less than 1 percent of lawyers were black. The same year, *The New York Age* reported that 80 percent of Harlemites were either unemployed or on work relief.

"I worked for one of the Communist newspapers when I was in college," said a Harlem physician. "I worked there during the 1940s. Nobody asked me what I thought about anything. They just wanted me to do the job they hired me to do. I was in college and needed

Sugar Ray Robinson (*fourth from right*), sitting next to Edna Mae Robinson. They are seated with unidentified guests, 1940s. *Courtesy of Ray Robinson II.*

some money. I saw a sign in their window. I walked up to the second floor and talked with them and they hired me."

"Along with the Communist females on the prowl, the lobby was the place for jitterbugs and hepsters to be seen," recalled trumpet player Joe Wilder. "But if you were going to be seen there, you had to look hip. We were against kinky hair in those days. We didn't have better sense. No way did any of us want any nappy hair. You know there was no pride in nappy hair in those days. We all wanted straight hair—we wanted people to think we had good hair. We bought the products to straighten our hair. It was a mixture with lye. Once it was put on, that lye would often burn our scalp and that was painful. It would pain us for days. It wasn't always pleasant, but once you combed it, your hair was definitely going to be straight. I wore my conk and most of the other musicians did too. When I look back, the white man was selling us that stuff to process our hair."

Those hair straightener products were flying off the shelves in drugstores. Ads belittling kinky hair appeared in a number of black newspapers throughout the early 1940s. [At the time, a *Pittsburgh Courier* ad read, "Kinky woolly hair is out of date. All hipsters in Harlem are using superior hair straightener. It's new sensational— the best large jar . . . $1 plus postage. Get Hip!"] There were but a very few musicians who didn't wear a conk in those days. Even the elegant Duke Ellington sported a conk.

"The zoot suit was the hippest outfit in those days for hipsters," said Joe Wilder. "Cab Calloway made the zoot suit a fad in the late 1930s. That zoot suit had the peg-leg pant that widened above the knee. Then there was the long coat with a hemline that hit around the knee. The zoot suits were definitely colorful too. Billy Eckstine wore a wide shirt collar. It was called the Billy Eckstine collar. Throw in the gold pocket watch with its long chain, a wide-brim hat, and a pair of sharp-toed gators that matched the zoot suit—that was the look. Then a girl was picked for the night."

Malcolm Little showed up in Harlem from Boston in 1942. Coming from Boston, his zoot suit wasn't up to Harlem's standards. He had an imitation that merely looked more or less like Cab Calloway's real thing. To complement his new sharkskin zoot suit, he strutted around Harlem in a pair of fancy Cadillac shoes—pointed-toed, orange-colored gators. He proudly wore his conked hairstyle.

"Girls in the hotel were never a problem," said businessman Nick Davis. "There was a new crop coming in all the time." "Some women on the make in the Theresa were taken advantage of and used for the most part by my musician friends," recalled Joe Wilder. "Those guys would take a two-dollar room in the hotel for a one-night affair. They had no intention of making the relationship permanent. They would use white women in such a terrible way as if they were trying to make up for all the lynchings that were going on, it seemed. But I guess I can't say that it was just that simple because they mistreated a whole lot of black women too. A number of musicians did it, both black and white. Some of the things they said they did to these women made me sick. Treated women like dirt. I asked them, 'Don't you have sisters?' They called me an Uncle Tom.

"Drugs were prevalent among musicians in those days. Mainly heroin and marijuana. They started on marijuana and then went to heroin. Coke wasn't around in the forties. Many of the musicians were badly treated by their managers. They didn't get paid commensurate with their talent. Those who used drugs often treated those who didn't like outcasts.

"Some of the musicians were married and on the road a lot. When they were home, they were in and out. Nothing was being paid into social security or pensions. No health insurance. Blacks in those days, for the most part, were day laborers. Not many of them lived to be old anyway. Guys like Duke, Cab, and the big orchestra leaders did all right for themselves. But many didn't. They ended up in bad shape.

"Lionel Hampton wasn't a nice person. He wasn't that fond of musicians. He was kind of arrogant. He had a lot of influence in the black and white communities. He could be contemptuous."

"A lot of musicians didn't like Lionel because his wife handled all the money," said musician Danny Moore. "Her name was Gladys.

She controlled everything. She paid all the musicians. She and Lionel were cheap. That's why nobody liked them."

"Lucky Millinder was good about paying musicians," said Joe
Wilder. "He was one of the few black bandleaders who paid a decent
salary. He even paid more than some of the better known orchestra
leaders. Maybe his past had a lot to do with it. He had a good business head. He was always fair. As a young boy in Chicago, he was a
runner and messenger for Al Capone and the mob."

There are stories in Harlem about Cab Calloway's hot temper.
Cab's band stayed in the Theresa unless they were on the road. Calloway is said to have fired Dizzy Gillespie after he and a few fellow
musicians got into trouble for throwing spitballs onstage. The two

Cab Calloway signing
autographs, 1940s.
Photograph by John W. Mosley.
Courtesy of the Charles L.
Blockson Afro-American
Collection, Temple University.

91

later made up. Lester Young, who had been with Cab for a while, lived in the hotel until he moved in with Billie Holiday.

"Louis Armstrong was friendly when he came in the Theresa's bar," recalled Joe Wilder. "Once he came into the hotel and started to talk about why people thought of him as an Uncle Tom. But Louis would say, 'Pops gets accused of being a Tom, but where I came from, if you were black and didn't smile, that could mean real trouble.' I almost had tears in my eyes when I heard Louis talk about his background and how he dealt with racism. He was a nice man and a gentleman."

The switchboard operator's station in the lobby was behind the registration desk. "That was Miss Mattye Jean's spot. She was the switchboard operator during Mr. Scott's tenure," recalled a former hotel resident. "I used to sit with her at the switchboard many late nights to keep her company. Mattye Jean was raised in Texas and attended Howard University. She was a classy lady—she came from a good family. She had a beautiful voice! She was a trained singer. Mattye was tall and slender with shoulder-length hair—very good-looking. She took leave from the hotel switchboard to perform in plays. When she traveled, I'd work the switchboard in her place. [James] Pork Chop Davis-Foreman was one the most famous hotel stepladder orators. Well, he was after Mattye Jean. I don't think she was interested in him at first. He was preaching all day in front of the Theresa, which meant he had no job. The merchants on Seventh Avenue and 125th Street and a few politicians like Adam Clayton Powell Jr. gave him pocket money. Pork Chop wasn't refined. He started calling her on the switchboard at night. He worried Mattye Jean to the point that she did begin seeing him. But secretly. I personally think that she was ashamed of him. His appearance was unkempt—and he wasn't particularly handsome."

"Look, Mattye Jean had an income," said a friend who knew Mattye Jean and Pork Chop. "He was no fool. He lived off Mattye Jean, especially once she became a teacher. Pork Chop could keep up his stepladder preaching—which he did. Later, he spoke at different rallies and participated in different boycotts in Harlem until he died in 1987. Mattye Jean gave him a nice funeral at Convent Avenue Baptist Church. All the big shots in Harlem turned out for him. Pork Chop stayed out on that ladder in front of the Theresa for years talking mean about the white man. Black politicians loved it because he was saying what they were afraid to even think about the white man and the white system in America. The politicians and business-people loved having him out there saying radical things about the white man."

"Pork Chop was talking so bad about the white man till I got scared," said Preston Wilcox. "Some people would come around and start looking around to see who was watching them. Pork Chop wasn't holding back. Them house Negroes would slip off because they didn't want to be seen around there listening to Pork Chop beat down the white man. He was calling him devilish even before Malcolm X came to town. Way back in the 1940s. Pork Chop was a disciple of Marcus Garvey. The black man gotta have some warrior in him. Pork Chop, Malcolm X, and Bumpy Johnson had warrior in 'em. Ain't none like that around today except maybe John Lewis."

Billy Rowe focused on the Theresa's switchboard operator in a 1946 column: "Theresa operator and secretary Mattye Jean is now back on duty since the return of the cast and chorus of *Shuffle*

Along. The USO Camp Show production of *Shuffle Along* recently returned from a ten-month European Tour. Cast members and directors Noble Sisle, Edgar Battle, Flournoy Miller, Johnny Lee, Jester Hairston are that happy to be back on the New York Scene."

Behind Mattye Jean's station was the hotel bar. There were two entrances to the bar. One entrance to the bar was the outside door next to the marquee. The other entrance was through the lobby. During the evenings, people crowded into the fifty-one-foot, J-shaped bar looking for sex, talking, networking, making business deals, or drinking. The bar was called the cocktail gathering place of high society. Described as "cheerfully noisy," the bar was equipped to take care of three-hundred people. It was always overflowing with crowds. Above the shelves of glasses and bottles was a pheasant's head that Walter Scott proudly claimed credit for catching. Mounted against the red-and-gold-striped wallpaper, the conspicuous animal head was the subject of conversation. The large mirrors behind the bar allowed beautiful ladies decked out in jewels and furs to admire themselves. The Theresa bar was to blacks what "Meet me under the clock at the Biltmore" was to whites.

"The bar was a crossroads where everybody stopped by during the day," said writer Albert Murray. "Duke, on his way downtown to his office in the Brill Building. Joe Louis. Editors and reporters from the *Amsterdam News*. Entertainment reporters, political reporters, anybody who wanted to know something about Harlem and what was going on in the black world."

"The bar was so crowded," said Billy Rowe, "a man could lose his pants and walk the length of the place without anybody noticing him."

John Thomas, the manager of the bar, and his seven bartenders wore white cloth coats. Usually two bartenders worked each shift. Thomas claimed that he had no need for bouncers because there were no problems with customers. "We hardly ever need them [bouncers]," he said. "If a guy gets too bad, we just ask him kindly not to come back."

"All the glasses from my bar are put in a sterilizer," said Walter Scott. "Something you don't see in most places in Harlem." Most of the regulars averaged two to three drinks. A shot of whiskey in those days was seventy-five cents. When the bar closed around two a.m., Walter Scott came down from his tenth-floor suite to collect the usual $400 from the bar's cash register.

"There were no barmaids," recalled Ruth Guzzman. "I don't think they were antiwomen, but the bartenders there didn't want us good-looking barmaids working with them because we'd get all those big tips. That just wasn't gonna happen."

By the mid-1940s, the hotel's reputation had become mythologized to the point that a number of black people in the country, especially young females looking for love, believed those who frequented the Theresa had money to burn.

"Earl [Maynard] and Hank were two of the bartenders that I remember," recalled Harlemite Marjorie Corbitt. "They were very protective of the young girls who hung around the bar."

They did their best to keep these naive girls away from cads who were coming on to them. This was often difficult because the girls had a goal—to hook a man with money. Many of these young ladies had made great sacrifices to raise the bus fare to get to New York and the $8 for one week's rent in the hotel. Earl and Hank could not have protected these determined young women no matter how hard they tried because they were set on being married to or at least being kept by their dream man. They were certain Prince Charming would walk into the bar, tap them on the shoulder, and they would ride off to a blissful life.

"There were women in the bar wearing foxes, minks—and some really loved beaver in those days too," recalled Ruth Guzzman. "They looked like movie stars or wealthy women. There was no way you could tell that they didn't have money. They had a polished look about them. But they were what I called ladies of the night. Believe me, it wasn't easy to accomplish that look. Not many woman could pull it off, either. Those who couldn't pull it off didn't hang out at the Theresa. They were down at the Braddock or at some other place, trying to get a hustle."

"Bojangles had a bad temper," recalled waitress Debbie McDade. "He loved Southern Comfort bourbon. He ordered it in the Theresa's bar all the time. I remember when he was performing at the Zanzibar Club downtown, he kept that brand of bourbon in his dressing room. Someone slipped into his dressing room and drank his bourbon one night and he went crazy. We got so scared. I remember that Pops [Louis Armstrong] was there and tried to calm him down. We all loved Pops."

"There were so many stories that circulated at the bar. There was the time a bunch of us musicians were sitting at the bar," recalled trumpet player Joe Wilder. "Everybody was talking about Billie Holiday. She was the star attraction in the Lucky Millinder band. They had played at the Earle Theater, a vaudeville theater in Philly. Billie had a court appearance in New York that she had missed or something. Two detectives went to Philly to the Earle Theater and she recognized them and ran. They chased her down Market Street and arrested her. She was a nice woman—good-hearted. Artie Shaw really liked Billie and he appreciated her talent. He took her on tour with his band quite often. They went all over the country. But Billie didn't take nothing from those whites when the band traveled down South. They'd say things to her like 'You old black nigger bitch,' and she'd yell back, 'You shut up, you old redneck son of a bitch.' She'd challenge them. And she wasn't afraid. It was her managers that got her hooked. They'd buy her a mink coat and then fill her up with drugs."

"It was Joe Glaser, her manager, who was feeding Billie Holiday drugs," said a longtime Harlem resident. "We all knew that."

"Lord, there was that quack doctor in the hotel," said Danny Moore. "Some of those old stories are coming back now. Some of those guys and girls could have died back then. That quack lived in the Theresa. I almost forgot about him. He was always hanging around the lobby wearing a white coat and had a stethoscope around his neck. I won't ever forget his name—Angelide Hyman. He spoke with a West Indian accent. We all trusted him like damn fools. He gave abortions to young girls in the hotel. Some of them ended up in the hospital. He was a butcher. There was one young girl who had a hysterectomy when she was in her early twenties after he messed her up. Looking back, we should have known that he was no real doctor. If one of the musicians came down with a gonorrhea, he gave them aspirin and told them it was penicillin. Somebody once told me that he was passing out Tums and claiming they were some kind of antibiotic drug to treat venereal diseases too. 'Swallow it real fast,' he

Billy Eckstine and Billie Holiday, 1940s. *Photograph by John W. Mosley. Courtesy of the Charles L. Blockson Afro-American Collection, Temple University.*

used to tell them. A lot of musicians thought he had cured them of venereal diseases. They would go back to him for more of his phony medicine—I guess it was mind over matter. These were the young cats. They didn't know any better. He had posed as a doctor for a number of years. We found out that he was some kind of orderly— something like that at a hospital in the city."

Amsterdam News writer James Booker had the bar regulars sitting on the edge of their seats when he talked about his near-death experience that had been instigated by the infamous gangster Bumpy Johnson.

James Booker recalled the scariest night of his life: "Late one night in the 1940s, Bumpy Johnson grabbed me outside the hotel and pressed a gun to my head. At the time Bumpy was on trial for racketeering and I was covering the story. Bumpy didn't like what he was reading about his trial in the newspaper and accused me of slanting his stories to please the white man. Another reporter, who was my friend, came upon the scene and pleaded with Bumpy to free me. I knew Bumpy. Yes, he has been romanticized in the movies lately. He was a madman—a common narcotics thug. All this talk about Bumpy being intelligent—being a great lover of literature. That's nonsense. He had spent so much time in so many prisons, what else could he do with all that time but read." The five-foot-seven-inch, deep-chocolate-colored, and dapper-dressing Johnson had been a resident of such New York prisons like Attica, Auburn, Clinton, and Ossining by the 1940s when the Theresa came into vogue. He was a pimp, a major numbers man, narcotics dealer, and an enforcer (this meant he beat up people). He was a Harlem legend during the 1930s and 1940s. A number of Harlemites feared him; and others despised him. By this time, he had been shot fifteen times, said the writer Helen Lawrenson. A number of people in Harlem thought Bumpy had been a plus for the community, believing that Harlem would have been in worse economic state had it not been for Bumpy's illegal enterprises.

"Bumpy used to buy us late-night dinners at Wells," recalled Debbie McDade. "When I got off work at the Theresa's counter, a group of us girls would go to Wells for dinner. Bumpy would come in and pick up the tab. If any guys tried to mess with us, he'd set them straight. I have only good memories of Bumpy Johnson. Bumpy loved to recite the great poets. He'd often write poetry and read it to us when he came in. It was very romantic."

"Had Bumpy been born white, he would have been a millionaire on Wall Street," declared Judge James Watson. "Bumpy was a very bright man. Nobody looked down on him to my knowledge when he came into the Theresa. He got the same respect as any lawyer or doctor. You have to remember, Bumpy was making thousands of dollars a day and employing a lot of people. Keeping people from getting evicted. He would threaten landlords who made trouble for tenants. So people felt some sense of obligation to him and they respected him for standing up for them."

"Bumpy Johnson wasn't in the league with my ex-husband Chink Cunningham," recalled Evelyn Cunningham. "Chink and I grew up together on Sugar Hill. He was a very smart man. Chink was partners with Johnny Walker. Chink and Johnny had permission from Dutch Schultz and Lucky Luciano to run the numbers racket in Harlem. Chink and Johnny were the successors to Harlem's biggest numbers man, Casper Holstein. Holstein was Harlem's foremost numbers banker in the 1920s. A native of the Virgin Islands, he was a patron of the Harlem Renaissance. It was no disgrace to be in the numbers business in those days. There were no jobs for black men with his talent. Smart black men had a certain pride. Take my parents. My mother was an extraordinary seamstress. She made a good living sewing for rich white ladies downtown. My father had a menial job. He was very smart. In those days it wasn't acceptable to some black men for their wives to make more money. I remember when one of the white ladies gave me money which was pay for my mother's work. I had to take the money straight to my mother. She'd tell me not to let my father know how much it was. She didn't want him to know how much she was getting paid. It was about his pride.

"Bumpy Johnson wasn't just into numbers. He was into drugs and pimping too. Now, that's very different from just being a numbers banker. When my husband introduced me to Bumpy, he said, 'I am going to introduce you to a real gangster.' There was the gangster Red Dillion. Dillion stabbed Chink. This is the way Chink explained it me. He walked up to Dillion and said, 'You owe me some money.' Red Dillion stabbed him in the back. Just like that."

"Red Dillion was married to a white woman we called Hillbilly Betty," recalled Danny Moore. "You know I say she was his wife. She was from Arkansas. Back in those days, nobody asked if you were married. If you were living with a woman, it was just left alone. Even today, we don't really know who's married unless we witness the marriage. Hillbilly Betty was Red Dillion's whore. She turned him on."

"There was the man who called himself Oscar Hammerstein who was always in the Theresa's bar," recalled Naidine Collins. "He was supposed to be a member of the famous Hammerstein family. He was a tall, white-looking man. If I remember correctly, he had some black blood in him. I think that's why he was the black sheep in the family. He lived in a hotel near Lenox Avenue in the One Forties. The hotel is still there. He was very bright. He knew a lot about politics, music, and poetry. We called him Oscar. He was a New York City greeter like Maceo Birch. He never paid for one drink in the Theresa. A bartender in the hotel almost lost his job for accepting money from Oscar for a drink."

"Oscar dated a friend of mine," added another former hotel resident. "He bought her a mink coat and took her to Europe. I met him in a bar with her. He didn't pay for drinks in any nightclub in Harlem. I don't know where he got his money. But he always had lots of money to spend on my friend. He stayed in Harlem until he got pretty old too. I knew him when he was older—in his fifties and sixties. The last time I saw him was in the 1960s."

Behind the bar, a set of doors led to the coffee shop, where red leather booths filled both sides of the walls. Above the booths, the walls were filled with photographs signed by celebrity greats. At the entrance of the coffee shop was a counter where customers were served.

"Certain customers preferred to eat at the counter while others sat in the booths," recalled former waitress Debbie McDade. "When Joe Louis was in the hotel, he came down almost every morning and ordered his usual mushroom omelet. The first time Jesse Owens came to the counter for breakfast I think he was disappointed because I didn't recognize him. He asked if I knew who he was and I said no. Of course, he was very nice about it. I always enjoyed his visits. He was very down-to-earth. One morning Bill [Bojangles] Robinson and Jesse Owens were in the coffee shop for hours. I overheard Jesse telling Bill Robinson about Hitler and his experience in the Olympics."

Bumpy Johnson was another regular in the coffee shop. Evelyn Cunningham recalled an incident about the gangster that took place there: "Bumpy came in and sat next to me. On this particular afternoon, there was a man who was pretty drunk sitting on the other side of me who accidentally spilled some coffee on my dress. I was a bit upset but didn't think the situation required Bumpy's interference.

Bumpy jumped to his feet and beat the poor man mercilessly. I thought he overdid it. But then you have to understand that Bumpy was a show-off."

That kind of behavior Bumpy displayed was all in a day's work for him. Helen Lawrenson recalled a similar incident: "We were standing at the bar in the Alhambra [theater and nightclub] when some luckless enemy came in. Bumpy moved like lightning, and the two men were down on the floor while the crowd shrank away from them. I watched them with fear and repulsion. It was not a pleasant sight. It was soon over and the inevitable loser, his eyes streaming from gouging, staggered out the door, barely able to make it. There was absolute silence in the room. Bumpy came and stood beside me again. 'Is my tie straight?' he asked."

"The high-class gangsters like Red Dillion, Bumpy Johnson, the Ross brothers, and Johnny Walker who came to the hotel didn't dress like the jitterbugs," said Debbie McDade. "They dressed like businessmen. They dressed in a conservative style. None of those zoot suits for them. In fact, Alabama Red wore a rose in his lapel every day. You could tell the pimp types. They wore flashy jewelry— the rings, the slick hairstyles. They drove flashy cars. But they all behaved in the hotel. There was never any trouble even from the ones who dressed like pimps."

Thurgood Marshall stopped in the coffee shop on his way to the NAACP offices on West Forty-third Street. He was a showstopper. By the 1940s, Marshall had become one of the best known and most beloved black lawyers in the country. Typically dressed in a stylish double-breasted suit with an impeccable white handkerchief in his breast pocket, he was Hollywood handsome.

"We couldn't take our eyes off him," recalled Debbie McDade. "Julia Scott, the manager of the coffee shop, used to wait on Mr. Marshall because she was afraid we'd spill coffee on him or cause some embarrassing accident because we were so nervous in his presence. 'You girls stop staring at Mr. Marshall,' she'd say when he came in. Mr. Marshall loved to tell jokes to the other men sitting at the counter. Sometimes we'd take a break, have a cup of coffee, and hear everything."

"Thurgood Marshall looked like a matinee idol," recalled longtime Harlemite Marjorie Corbitt. "He used to come to the Theresa to speak to women's groups, and they treated him like a movie star. He was handsome in those days."

Walter Scott had proudly served his country in World War I as a lieutenant in the 368th Infantry. For him, it was his patriotic duty to serve in the U.S. military. As the cash register rang constantly and the tunes blared from the jukebox in the coffee shop, black men in suits pressed hard their opinions on the war. A *Life* magazine article declared, "There is no place in the nation where civil defense is now a more burning topic than in Harlem." There were black nationalist types in the coffee shop making the point that black men and women should not fight for democracy abroad when America's democracy itself was fake. America, in her blatant hypocrisy, was expressing outrage over the persecution of oppressed peoples in Europe while the horror of lynching was searing the fabric of its own country.

Nearly seven hundred thousand black Americans were in the armed services during World War II. A law enforced by the Selective Service Act of 1940 made the presence of one black for every nine men inducted into the military a standard. Essentially, all black soldiers served in segregated units, but under white leadership.

"When I returned from the army, I headed straight for the Hotel Theresa," said Judge James Watson. "I knew that I could find out all I needed to know in the Theresa bar. I could catch up on all that had happened while I was away. I was using a cane because my leg had been injured. I was in uniform. I was a bit taken aback by the scorn I received from some of my old buddies that were in the hotel. They were now members of the Communist Party or they were black nationalists. They chastised me for going into the white man's army. They looked at my injured leg and really became even more hostile. They couldn't understand why I served in the military—put my life on the line for a country that treated blacks like second-class citizens. I really didn't get angry with them because I understood where they were coming from.

"When Joe Louis joined the army, it surprised everyone in the Theresa," remembered Judge James Watson. "Not because Joe wasn't patriotic. But he loved being in the ring so much, and we figured he'd miss the ring."

Joe Louis stepped from his chauffeur-driven limousine in 1942 at Camp Upton in New York, to enlist in the army. There was no recognition of his status as a universal celebrity. In his typical nonchalant manner, he put it this way: "They gave me my uniform and sent me over to the colored section."

A. Philip Randolph stopped at the counter on a number of evenings during 1941. He was using the office space on the mezzanine level in the hotel for his planned march on Washington demanding the federal government end its discrimination in hiring.

That same year, President Franklin Roosevelt signed Executive Order 8802, which banned Jim Crow hiring policies by defense-related businesses that held federal contracts. Roosevelt's signing of this order was a direct result of Randolph's efforts. Theresa resident and activist Anna Arnold Hedgeman was among Randolph's committee members.

On a number of evenings Randolph met NAACP leaders Walter White and Roy Wilkins in the hotel coffee shop to discuss the war and his planned march. Benjamin Davis was often there. Randolph and Davis agreed that black men must disregard potential recruiting laws and refuse military service unless a policy of integration was enforced. NAACP integrationists like Walter White and Roy Wilkins argued on behalf of a moderate stance on blacks enlisting in the military. At the time, the NAACP was demanding from the federal government a complete removal of Jim Crow units. White and Wilkins advocated that black men and women serve their country but try to institute change.

As the war dragged on, Europe was still being devastated. Americans had become accustomed to rationing. They were limited to three pairs of shoes a year, and less than thirty ounces of meat per week. But life at the Theresa hadn't changed much. The regulars at the bar were drinking and eating as much as ever. A number of the hotel regulars like Joe Louis, Sugar Ray Robinson, Rex Ingram, and Gordon Parks were in the military. But the gossips in the hotel bar were whispering that the Theresa's most famous resident was an adornment for the United States Army. Especially after reading in Billy Rowe's column that the champ, who had recently been stationed in California, would appear in the big-screen version of Irving Berlin's hit play *This Is the Army*.

Sugar Ray Robinson and
Edna Mae Robinson, 1940s.
Courtesy of Ray Robinson II.

While Sugar Ray Robinson was in the army, he and the former
Cotton Club showgirl Edna Mae Holly had tongues wagging in the
hotel when they got hitched in Chicago in 1943. "Edna Mae was
simply gorgeous," recalled Delilah Jackson, a chronicler of Harlem's
entertainment history for several decades. "All the men would stare

and whistle at her when she walked down the street. She was every black man's dream with her light skin, long hair that hung down her back, and her beautiful legs. I know many a man who would have thought they were in heaven to have her by the arm strolling down 125th Street. The way she sashayed, throwing her shapely hips, she knew she was something special. I guess she had every reason to be vain. You could tell by the expression on her face that she loved people noticing her. When I was with her, she loved showing off her legs. Even when she performed almost nude in Connie's Inn in 1932 when she was sixteen or seventeen, she was proud of her body. She used to show me pictures of her dressed in nothing at all. I have to admit that she had a fantastic body. But she also had class, culture, and sophistication." The twenty-one-year-old boxer Robinson had married a woman seven years his senior. The newlyweds checked into an eleventh-floor suite in the Hotel Theresa. Gossips in the hotel sniggered about the age difference between the bride and the groom. "Ray's mother didn't want him to marry her because she was so much older than he was," recalled Delilah Jackson. The Holly family wasn't pleased with the marriage either. They saw Ray Robinson as an unlettered boxer who had married way above himself into the prestigious Holly family. "Edna Mae is fourth generation of college-bred member of our family," scoffed her aunt Blanche Holly. "Doctors and lawyers. And her great-grandfather came out of slavery and graduated from Harvard, studied ministry, and was the first Negro to be consecrated a bishop in the United States. The Right Reverend James Theodore Holly, an Episcopal bishop." The news wasn't all bad for Ray Robinson's groupies. He was no longer a bachelor, but marriage was simply a minor nuisance for him and his paramours.

Leaving Edna Mae behind in the Theresa, Ray Robinson returned to his duties as a soldier. The year the Robinsons married, Edna Mae and a number of hotel residents witnessed the Harlem riots from their windows. It all started in the sleazy Braddock Hotel on 126th Street and Eighth Avenue. A policeman, James Collins, was stationed in the hotel lobby because of past trouble in the Braddock. When a drunken female became loud and disorderly, the policeman tried to arrest her. A black military policeman named Robert Bandy was on the scene. When Collins tried to physically restrain the out-of-control female, Bandy grabbed Collins's nightstick and hit him in the head. As Bandy tried to flee the scene, Collins shot him in the shoulder and placed him under arrest. A number of Harlemites in the streets were saying that a white cop had shot a black man to death in cold blood in the Braddock Hotel. Rumors spread around Harlem as fast as lightning. Blacks began rioting in the streets.

Jewel Sims Okala remembered the scene: "When I returned to Harlem from Great Barrington, Massachusetts, by train at the 125th Street station, that's when I realized there was trouble. I got in the car with Jack Nail [John E. 'Jack' Nail was a successful Harlem real estate mogul and the brother-in-law of James Weldon Johnson] at the station and he yelled, 'Get down!' Rocks, bricks, debris, and glass were flying everywhere. I stayed down on the floor of the car until we got to the Theresa. It was really scary. We could see a lot of the disturbance from our windows in the hotel." When the riot was over, six black men had been killed by white policemen. A number of blacks were injured.

•   •   •

Upstairs from the Theresa lobby, the mezzanine was comfortably filled with overstuffed, garnet-colored sofas and tables for cocktails. Guests used this space for relaxation and informal meetings. The oatmeal-colored club room was on this level. It had dark venetian blinds covering the long windows, with a number of small, square tables used for bridge, meetings, small dinners, and parties. Walter Scott asked popular jazz singer and lyricist Una Mae Carlisle to perform in the club room when there was a special occasion for hotel employees and for staff holiday parties. Una Mae, who sang with Fats Waller, spent the last years of the 1930s performing solo and recording in Europe. The Xenia, Ohio, native returned to New York in 1940. She recorded such hits as "Stardust," "I Can't Give You Anything but Love," and "Walkin' by the River," The usually cool Walter Scott swayed his body and tapped his feet to Una Mae's luscious voice. During these occasions, the pipe-smoking manager couldn't stop himself from pressing against the piano while gazing into the eyes of the petite, pretty Una Mae Carlisle. Walter Scott enjoyed sharing the piano bench with the her and singing along with the jazz diva.

"Walter Scott loosened up when Una Mae played the piano and sang," said Naidine Collins. "His wife, Gertrude, was a short frump with a thick body. She never came to the employees' parties. Walter Scott always asked Una Mae to sing when he gave a party for the hotel workers. There was nothing going on between Walter Scott and Una Mae. She was involved with musician Johnny Bradford. Mr. Scott was a gentleman through and through."

Etienne Johnson's boutique, on the mezzanine level, was one of Harlem's most popular and pricey shops. Etienne, the owner, was a tall, elegant lady with a supermodel's figure. The Columbia, South Carolina, native outfitted a number of the great celebrities of the era—Josephine Baker, Lena Horne, Ella Fitzgerald, Sarah Vaughan.

"That was the boutique for Harlem's upper class," recalled Evelyn Cunningham. "Etienne was a classy lady. She had great dignity. She had the nicest boutique in Harlem in those days. Her merchandise was picked out carefully."

"Etienne got to know her regular customers—she knew our taste," recalled Jewel Sims Okala. "She dressed so exquisite, all in the hotel had such confidence in her taste. There were times when I'd tell her that I was going to a particular affair, she knew exactly what to select for me. She helped me select my wedding dress. Her husband was often around. He'd stop by the boutique and help her unpack new stock. They were very close. At some point he left his job and worked with her full-time in the boutique. He was a rather courtly man."

"When I was in high school, I loved coming to the Theresa," recalled retired nurse Joan Fairservis. "My mother had friends who lived in the hotel. When I visited mom's friends, who lived on the seventh floor, I'd stop down on mezzanine to browse in Etienne's before going home. I started taking my friends there after school. She had nice clothes even for young girls."

"There was a barbershop in the Theresa on the mezzanine level," recalled Danny Moore. "There were two barbers in there. One's name was Murdock. He was on junk. But he could put a mean conk in your hair. Everybody wanted Murdock to put their conk in even when he was stoned. One time I went in there and Murdock was putting the conk in Cannonball Adderley's hair."

The Black National Newspaper Publishing Association had an office on the second floor. "We had a nice office with a view that looked out on Seventh Avenue and 124th Street, which was the back of the hotel," recalled James Booker. "Billy Rowe of the *Pittsburgh Courier* and Major Robinson of the *Chicago Defender*, and later *Jet*, often stopped by the association's office in the hotel. This office was especially useful to out-of-town reporters. They stayed at the Theresa because it was the leading place to make contacts and get stories. The office was useful for writing stories. Still, the bar was the best place to be. Nobody wanted to miss a scoop. Bartenders, elevator workers, and maids were all great about providing scoops to reporters because they always knew who was staying in the hotel."

The elegant orchid dining room was managed by Willette Crane. It was one of the hotel's most beautiful areas. Sophisticated orchid and canary decor made the dining room a tranquil setting for the many banquets and receptions that were held there. The room was arranged to suit the occasion. For formal banquets, tables were arranged in a long, rectangular style to seat ten to twelve guests each. Numerous smaller tables were used for intimate dinners. The Hotel Theresa's trademark white linen cloths and daily fresh flowers that reflected in the radiant mirrored walls created a double pleasure, and an inviting and elegant decor.

The orchid dining room was Walter Scott's pride and joy when it came to rooms in the hotel. He only permitted Harlem's high society and intellectuals to host literary parties and dinners in the orchid dining room. When *Native Son* was released, there in the orchid room Richard Wright's masterpiece was celebrated by Harlem's elite authors and artists, including Langston Hughes, Ralph Ellison, and artists Romare Bearden, Aaron Douglas, and Ellen Tarry. In 1946, friends of the new author Ann Petry threw a lavish literary party to honor her new book, *The Street.* Harlem society in attendance were Roberta Bosley, Grace Nail Johnson, John Henrik Clarke, Harold Jackman, Robert Weaver, Dorothy West, and the Henry Lee Moons. That same year, local Harlem authors attended a dinner hosted by Harold Guinzburg, president of Viking Press, in honor of Ellen Tarry's book *My Dog Rinty.* Singer Josh White performed for guests including Gladys and Walter White, Louis T. Wright, and Carl Van Vechten.

"We had the James Weldon Johnson literary group in the 1940s," recalled the late historian John Henrik Clarke. "We met in the orchid dining room occasionally at the hotel for a meeting. At one point, I was the only man in the group. There were about a dozen of us—Johnson's widow, Ellen Tarry, Roberta Bosley, and some others. Then Harold Jackman asked if he could join the group. So we didn't know too much about him personally. We did know he was educated and a very sophisticated person. The single women got all excited. Here was an eligible bachelor coming into our group. Here comes Jackman to the next meeting, and the women quickly realized that he wasn't interested in women period."

Meals were cooked in a kitchen located one floor above the orchid dining room. The hotel's dinner menu featured steaks, ham, fried and baked chicken, fried or baked fish, baked potatoes, macaroni and cheese, string beans, turnip and collard greens, rice, gravy, biscuits, corn bread, and an array of desserts. The dining room's fanciful Christmas menu was a hit with residents. The cook prepared turkey with trimmings and the hotel's regular dinner menu. A number of residents complained about the food being cold by the time it reached them in the dining room.

"The food served from the kitchen was often overcooked. I stopped eating there," recalled Naidine Collins. "I heard the steaks were fairly good." Billy Rowe agreed. He too found at least one offer on the menu to his satisfaction. In a 1941 column, he wrote, "The best steak in town since the 'Mimo Special' [Mimo was a Harlem nightclub that was no longer in business] can be had at the Theresa."

"Most of the time, I ate down the street on Seventh Avenue at Frazier's," recalled Naidine Collins. "Lord, Mamie could cook her butt off. Nobody in Harlem can come close to cooking as good as Mamie. She served collard greens, candied sweet potatoes, fried chicken, ham, corn bread—the usual soul food or Southern-style menu. Frazier's was elegant. Nice tablecloths—fresh flowers. Mamie Frazier wouldn't have it any other way. That's where you saw all the big-shot celebrities from the hotel. It was that kind of place. Frazier's Restaurant was known as the gourmet paradise. The crowds that gathered there. It was difficult to get a seat sometimes.

"Sidney Poitier and his partner—we called him Red. Can't remember his last name. They had a barbecue joint on 137th and Fifth. We used to go there and eat. Sometimes, they delivered barbecue ribs to the hotel.

"I cooked on a hot plate in my room," recalled Naidine. "The elevator man—I forget his name—he used to bring me ice from the bar every day to keep my food fresh. In the wintertime, I'd put my food on the fire escape. We weren't suppose to cook in our rooms, but a few of the guests did."

Suites with sitting rooms in the Theresa cost $8 per day. The suites had a bedroom with standard bedroom accessories—double bed, dressers, armoires, and comfortable chairs. A bathroom and sitting room completed the suite. Graduate students attending Columbia and New York universities and nurses who worked in neighboring hospitals lived in the cheaper rooms. Bathrooms for the cheaper rooms were communal. Hotel residents could entertain their guests in common areas—or more discreetly in their suites and rooms.

In 1944, the writer Zora Neale Hurston took a single room in the Theresa. She was in the midst of a divorce and lived in the Theresa for several months while finishing the play *Polk County*. She collaborated on the musical with Dorothy Waring.

Society ladies who lived in the hotel the year-round included Florence Murray, editor of the *Negro Yearbook*; Ally Simms, aunt of the cartoonist E. Simms Campbell; Anna Arnold Hedgeman, a New York activist; Gertrude Scott, the manager's wife; Jewel Sims Okala; businesswoman Rose Morgan; and Grace Nail Johnson. Historically, upperclass blacks have been ignored by whites of equal status and distanced by the less illustrious of their race. These ladies of social prominence believed that black people of high class kept their social affairs away from the rest of the world, white and black, to the extent that they could. They made their personal standards as high as possible and expected no less from others in their tight circle. They visited one another and kept a strict and guarded line drawn about themselves in the Theresa.

Contact between the hipster class and the hotel society was unavoidable in the public areas in the hotel, the hallways, elevators, coffee shop, lobby. So, the society ladies didn't go into the hotel bar.

"It was awkward living under the same roof with certain types that came to the hotel, particularly when there was a Joe Louis fight

Grace Nail Johnson, 1940s.
Courtesy of Sondra Kathryn Wilson.

in New York," recalled Jewel Sims Okala. "We'd smell marijuana in the hallways. We could also hear loud sounds—people making love—that we sometimes heard in the hallway. Some of the guests were a nightmare for Mr. Scott. When he learned about it, he'd immediately ask the disruptive parties to pack and leave the hotel. He didn't tolerate that awful behavior. We just stayed away from that element. A few of the folks who lived there would ask my husband and me to stop in their suite for drinks. We accepted no invitations from them for anything. There was no socializing or getting chummy with them. There was Anna Arnold Hedgeman and a few others we chatted with, however. We saw Mr. [Joe] Louis in the hotel often, but we made no effort to get friendly with him. Mr. Scott was definitely deferential to Grace Nail Johnson and all of his distinguished guests. He placed his special guests on certain floors.

"Ollie Harrington, the cartoonist, was a friend of ours. We used to visit with him in the coffee shop. He had a popular newspaper cartoon character called Bootsie. He'd work in the coffee shop on Bootsie quite often."

"Grace Nail Johnson's cousin Frances Cohen came to the hotel sometimes," recalled Naidine Collins. "She and Mrs. Johnson looked like sisters rather than cousins. People in the hotel knew that Mrs. Cohen was passing for white. She and Mrs. Johnson became reaquainted after her husband died. That's really when she started coming to Harlem. Her husband was a very rich, Jewish businessman. They lived on East Fifty-seventh Street. She had not been around her family for a long time. We weren't sure if he ever knew that she was black. She'd visit the hotel about once a week to see Mrs. Johnson. They ate in Frazier's. I guess Frances Cohen was glad to get back to her black roots. I'd see her and Mrs. Johnson walking along Seventh Avenue. Folks in the hotel said they would see Mrs. Cohen and Mrs. Johnson shopping downtown on Fifth Avenue and neither of them would speak. Around the Theresa folks used to say that once Mrs. Johnson got on that Fifth Avenue bus to head downtown, when the bus hit 110th Street, she didn't speak to any black people from Harlem.

"Walter Scott would patrol the halls more often when there was a Joe Louis event in New York. He was like a prison guard," added Naidine. "His gait was slow. I can see him now walking up and down those halls late at night. I could smell his pipe smoke. Mr. Scott seemed old to me back then because I was maybe nineteen or so.

Looking back, he was probably in his forties. He had better not smell reefer in the hallways. If he did, he'd evict the person."

"Walter Scott and his assistants were all doing their job," recalled Danny Moore. "I didn't see any of those upper-class types in the hotel. I guess I was too busy with my music. Some of the musicians were on junk in the hotel because they thought it would make 'em play better. It was mostly marijuana and heroin. Then, there was the frustration of so much damn talent—so much damn rare talent in the Theresa. The way it makes an artist feel when he knows he's damn good. He's better at playing the blues—jazz. Then he gets mistreated because of race discrimination. That shit is hard to cope with. Sometimes junk was the answer. There was Fats Navarro, the great trumpet player. Fats was from Key West, Florida. When he came to New York, he lived in the Theresa for a while in 1945. When he first arrived at the Theresa, he weighed over three hundred pounds. Fats caught tuberculosis and he was on junk. He died at twenty-seven, weighing a little over one hundred pounds. He played with all the greats like Billy Eckstine, Illinois Jacquet, and Coleman Hawkins.

"There ain't gonna never be another Charlie Parker. Not ever. He was the greatest sax player ever. He was on junk all the while, and he was still the best. This happened later, but just like when Little Willie John recorded 'Fever' in 1956, two years later Peggy Lee made it a hit. It was her version that went to the top of the charts. Peggy Lee couldn't sing like Little Willie John. Everybody in the Theresa and all over Harlem were talking about how those white producers who came uptown sneaking around the Apollo Theater and recording black material and then, you'd hear a white singer on the radio singing the same song. That would put anybody on junk."

A number of Harlemites have talked about the history of black music and whites stealing on countless occasions. For example, when the ragtime craze swept the world as American music, some whites tried to steal credit for originating it. Even today in Harlem, many black people are firm in their belief that it is an old trick of the white race that, as soon as anything created by blacks is acclaimed as great, they set out to steal it.

"Duke Ellington didn't tolerate drugs in his orchestra," said Danny Moore. "He was a class act. If someone was on drugs, Duke had a way of making them feel so bad, they'd leave. Blacks in those days, for the most part, were day laborers. Some of them didn't live to old age. Guys like Duke, Cab, and the big orchestra leaders did all right for themselves. But many didn't. They ended up in bad shape."

"Musicians were shooting up thinking it would make them able to play all night," said emcee Hal Jackson. "They did play all night, but at a terrible cost to their bodies. With so many handicaps, dope was one that we could do without."

There were four hundred black hotels across America in 1946. A group of hotel owners compiled a list of musicians, singers, writers, and professional people who were called rent jumpers. The list was distributed to all black-based hotels across the nation. Rent jumpers had to pay in advance.

"Once, I got my door jammed for not paying rent," said Danny Moore. "It was no big deal. I hadn't paid rent, so I wasn't going to get ugly with management about it. The hotel kept your belongings until you paid."

Not everybody was happy with the Theresa. The 1946 *Ebony* article noted some of the hotel's flaws: "dimly lit dingy, ancient furnishings, and limited room service." The article quoted "a lovely young woman's conversation, overheard in the mezzanine . . . 'How much longer are they going to treat us as if we had never seen any place nicer than the Theresa? How much longer they going to pass off good-enough on us when we deserve the best? I've passed downtown—a thousand of us have gone to conferences and appeared at benefits in New York's white hotels; we can pay for what we saw there—space and beauty, well-cooked, original food, shaded lights, color in the rooms, a flower on the table—you'd think there weren't any good cooks or decorators in Harlem. Why don't they hire them to work at the Theresa?' The older woman answered, 'Just be patient, dearie. It's the war that made them go so slow. And you have to realize this is a small hotel, and not many of the rooms are big enough to call for an $8 rent. It may be where the most famous of our race stay, but it's a small hotel for that, and not very rich. Besides, we didn't build it with funny lights and tiled floors. We didn't put in this dusty statue,' she gestured at a coy plaster maiden, dressed apparently in a longish rayon union suit and a sun bonnet, 'or make the outside fancy so it would catch all the dirt in Harlem as it blows by. This was a white hotel, honey. Mr. Scott's only been here six years.' "

Why would a place that housed so many talented musicians rely on a jukebox for musical entertainment? The musicians who were year-around residents included the likes of Paul Williams, Lucky Millinder, and Cab Calloway. The club room, the bar, and the grill were each outfitted with a jukebox, but their clashing songs couldn't be heard above the noisy conversations and the clacking sounds of ice in the cocktail mixers. Why was there no dance floor? one guest wondered. Hotel guests complained about the beauty shop. The curtains that divided each booth were haphazardly hanging on iron pipes. Another guest said to a reporter, "Bad as that might be, this is a million times better than any other joint in Harlem, and I don't want to get in bad here for shooting my face. After all, I gotta have a place to sleep." It was well known that the Theresa was often booked three months in advance. Once when there was a Joe Louis fight in New York, it took Buddy Young of New York Yankee fame five hours to get a room in the hotel.

The Theresa represented a utopia for thousands of blacks from the rural South and other parts of the country. Dream chasers viewed it as the ideal setting to reinvent themselves. They could pretend to be anyone they desired, if only for a short time. A number of the Theresa's guests built their lives on a foundation of fabrication. And the Theresa played a role in keeping those dreams alive; it was a stage for dreamers and wannabes.

"There is no doubt that the hotel was romanticized by certain writers," recalled *Amsterdam News* reporter James Booker. "A few of the columnists who wrote about the hotel, I think they exaggerated its amenities and the wealth of its guests. I knew all the writers of that era. That was their personality. A few of them wrote about the hotel in a way that made it sound more impressive than it was. People came to New York believing everything they had read about the Theresa. I saw the bar as a place for hard news. I wasn't interested in glamour and society news. My interest was not show people."

A number of people recalled one young lady who came to the hotel in search of a future filled with fame, love, and money: Betty Stanton. She arrived at the hotel in the 1940s, at the age of seventeen. Both men and women who recall her agree that she was a "beige" beauty—long black hair, long legs, and an hourglass figure that stopped traffic on Seventh Avenue. Of course, Betty's dream was to catch a wealthy man. It didn't matter whether the prospect was in entertainment, medicine, law, or business—she wanted a prominent man. She was estranged from her poverty-stricken family (who had moved from rural Georgia to Baltimore only a few years before her arrival in New York). Her whereabouts were unknown to them.

"My family thought I was in Chicago," recalled Betty Stanton. "A friend from Baltimore went to live in Chicago the same time that I came to New York. She didn't want her family to know where she was either. I sent my letters for my family to her in Chicago, and she mailed them on to Baltimore. The postmark was Chicago, so that my family would believe that I was really living there. She sent me letters to mail to her family so that they would believe that she lived in New York. It was years before I let my family know that I was in New York."

Being a light-skinned woman, Betty was hired by Blumstein's Department Store as a salesgirl. Her wardrobe from Blumstein's and her proximity to upper-class women who frequented the hotel enabled her to imitate their style and manner. To enhance her purse, she did print modeling for Lucky Gold cigarettes.

Betty's deceased grandmother had been in long-term domestic service for a wealthy black Georgia couple. The couple's two sons were prominent in Harlem by the time Betty arrived at the Theresa. One son was an attorney and the other a physician. Exploiting her grandmother's relationship with the wealthy family, she cast herself as the niece of the brothers. They didn't deny her story, but they never acknowledged her as kin. The brothers' wives refused to associate with her. Their conspicuous snub did raise some questions among some in the hotel. Still, attending many of the most elite soirees in the company of some of Harlem's most eligible bachelors, Betty presented herself as a Baltimore socialite. Newspaper accounts about Harlem society cited her as a Baltimore debutante, and a relative of the prominent attorney and physician. Dating actors, sports figures, musicians, and doctors, she kept her facade intact for a couple of years. But with each affair her reputation became more sordid. The brothers' wives became increasingly embarrassed and enraged by this fallen woman claiming family ties.

"When Betty was raped, that ended her cover," recalled a Harlemite who knew Betty. "She was always calling older doctors in Harlem her uncles. All of us who knew her thought it was strange that she wanted to relate to these doctors like family. Late one night she was supposed to be meeting a doctor whom she was dating. While waiting outside his office—he had an office in a building on Seventh Avenue—a man grabbed her and forced her into the basement of the apartment building, where he raped her. The rape was in the papers. I don't think they ever found out who raped Betty."

After the rape, the wives of the two brothers made her lineage known throughout Harlem. One of the men who remembered Betty said, "I really had no problem with these relationships between these girls looking for wealthy men. These things were always two-way. But many hearts were broken, including Betty's."

"There was one doctor who really loved Betty," said a friend. "Although once when I was visiting in the hotel, and she was out, he tried to hit on me. He was from a socially prominent family. His mother was against Betty because she had no college degree. Had Betty been educated, I think he would have married her. But she couldn't fit into that society circle. The doctor eventually married a doctor's daughter. She was a registered nurse. He continued to see Betty after he married."

"I saw Betty Stanton the other day," recalled a longtime Harlem resident. "I stopped in to visit a friend who lives in her building. I hadn't seen her in a while so I decided to pay her a brief visit. I couldn't believe the way she's living—a house full of dogs and old photographs covering the walls. Every space is covered with pictures from her old showgirl and modeling days. The dogs were all over the apartment and the place smelled like piss. My heart cried for her. I know about all the men in her life and her heart being broken over and over. It's made me so sad because all that had to have taken a toll on her. I had no idea that she was living like that. I called another friend to find out what we could do for her. It bothered me for days."

Like Betty Stanton, Baron Smith was a pretender who came to the Theresa each summer in the 1940s from Nassau. Smith was tall, burly, brown-skinned man—who weighed over three hundred pounds. He loved to profile and style in the hotel lobby in his numerous white, double-breasted suits. His panama hat would be tilted toward the front of his head. An elegant dresser, his wardrobe of tailor-made suits was impressive. Beneath his well-crafted facade was a desperate wannabe. For one week each summer in the hotel, Smith cast himself as a dashing, rich Casanova.

"Baron Smith's image and presence were tailor-made fabrication," recalled Sidney Poitier. "The real life of the real Baron Smith was set in Nassau, Bahamas. There he was a barkeeper who sold rum to the locals. His profit margin had to ignore other obligations in order to cover his seven-day pilgrimage to [the Theresa] each summer. And each summer, this man of substance would return to be eagerly received by the hotel's management and staff . . . including certain ladies of the night. I learned much from Harlem's generosity in welcoming Baron Smith with his image as a man of importance, wealth, generosity, and presence—all fashioned with clothing and pretense—and its generosity in keeping such dreams alive for Baron Smith and dreamers like him from all over the world."

"Baron Smith told us that he was something like a big, important diplomat from the Caribbean," recalled Debbie McDade. "We always believed that about him. He'd spend money like he was rich. Taking girls out on the town. Everybody looked forward to his visits."

"Americans are victims of a confused legacy," according to clinical psychologist Paula Owens. "This confusion manifests itself within every culture and at every social stratum." This confusion was displayed in a number of ways. Ora, a hotel resident, displayed confusion around skin color.

Ora, a tall, brown-skinned woman in her late teens, came to the hotel in 1943 from North Carolina. Like a number of others, the drama of her troubled legacy played itself out in the hotel. Her dream was to be a chorus girl.

"It was a big deal to be a chorus girl in New York in the 1940s," said barmaid Ruth Guzzman. "You had to be light-skinned," said Danny Moore. "You had to be damn near white-looking. That was definitely a must."

Girls were flocking to New York every day in search of fame as a dancer in one of Harlem's famous niteries. Most of them didn't make the cut. The next best opportunity was to be a barmaid or cigarette girl. For a number of young women, any job in a night club that placed them near celebrities and the great musicians, was better than cleaning toilets in a white lady's house. Ora had a heavy mane of long black hair. She was a beautiful woman, but she wasn't going to make the cut as a chorus girl because her skin was brown.

"Ora lived on my floor," recalled Jewel Sims Okala. "One night she was standing in her doorway. I had to pass her door to get to my suite. She introduced herself and we talked briefly. I was struck by that fact that she was literally covered from head to toe in bleaching cream. She told me that she wanted to be a dancer, but had been unsuccessful because her skin was too dark. As a nurse, I was afraid of the possible skin damage that the bleaching cream could cause. Ora was obsessed with making her skin lighter. There were jars and jars of bleaching cream stacked on her dresser. After that night, she'd stop me in the hallway and put her hand against mine. 'Am I getting any lighter?' she'd ask. It made no sense to me. I told her to forget being a chorus girl and get an education. She was a fool."

Ora wasn't alone in her obsession with light skin. Jars of bleaching creams were flying off the shelves on drugstores around Harlem. Ads for bleaching cream were abundant in black newspapers. A 1940s ad read, "If your skin has become darker, coarse, or reddened and your appearance worries you, makes you sad, if you are being neglected by your friends, loved ones, get a Revoline Bleach cream and you will quickly regain romance, love, popularity." Another ad read, "Is your face as fashionably light, lovely and smooth looking as you want it? If not try White's Specific Face Cream (bleach), a skin ointment used by thousands—and see for yourself what a difference it makes." Other skin-whitener ads promised jobs, love, and even money.

"Ora used to dress up on Friday and Saturday nights," recalled former Harlemite and nurse Mary Pitman. "She wore beautiful, expensive clothes. She'd tell everybody that she saw that she was going out with some famous celebrity or this doctor or that lawyer. She'd go in and out of our rooms to show off her clothes. The sad story is that there was no date. She'd get all dressed up and stay in her room. She never talked about the date the following day, at least not to me. We just figured out that there was really no date."

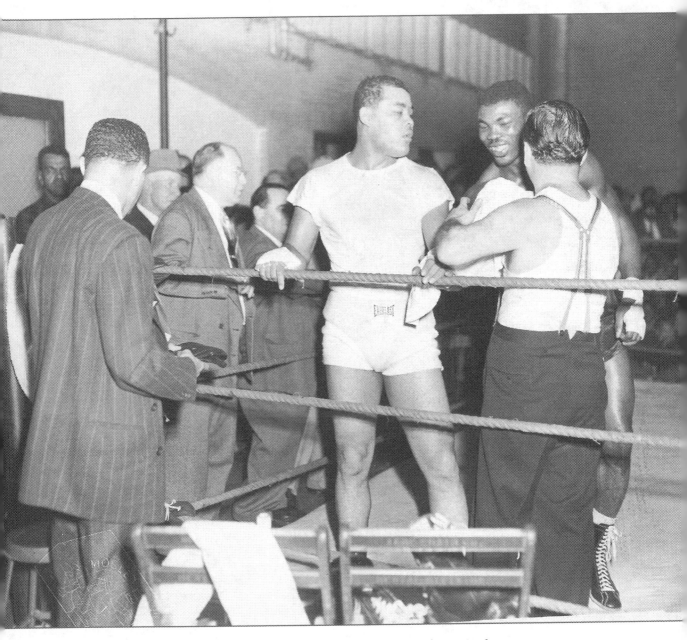

Joe Louis in training, 1940s. *Photograph by John W. Mosley.*
Courtesy of the Charles L. Blockson Afro-American Collection, Temple University.

Seven

THE JOE LOUIS ERA

T he Joe Louis era is the era of the Theresa," said writer Albert
Murray. "Not only did black America throng to the hotel," but
Louis usually kept two suites reserved there for himself. A Joe Louis
fight was circus time in Harlem. Not since the celebrated champion
Jack Johnson was there such a phenomenal prizefighter—black or
white. His successive wins in the boxing ring coincided with the
Great Depression, which hit Harlem particularly hard. "There were
no jobs in those days for black men with skills," recalled Evelyn Cunningham. Harlemites suffered discrimination in housing, education, jobs. "Neither Father Divine, with his free banquets for blacks,
nor Franklin Roosevelt, with his New Deal, managed to lift the spir-
its of suffering Harlemites as much as Joe Louis did," said the writer
Jervis Anderson. It's easy, therefore, to understand why black
America's pride in Joe Louis was excessive.

Joe Louis was born in Alabama and moved to Detroit as a
teenager. In 1935, twenty-one-year-old Louis married seventeen-
year-old Chicagoan Marva Trotter in Harlem. Louis was a serial phi-
landerer though, so their marriage was destined to be rocky
throughout its existence.

"Joe's managers, John Roxborough and Julian Black, were very distinguished men who came from upper-class black Detroit families," said musician James Michaels. "They knew Joe was rough around the edges. Marva Trotter came from that kind of background that Roxborough and Black shared. She could give Joe some class. At least that's what they hoped."

Mobbed by throngs of fans when he hit the streets of Harlem, he never tired of seeing those who were so proud of him. "There was nothing conceited about Joe," recalled his second wife, Rose Morgan. "He loved people and he was nonchalant about his celebrity. When we married in 1955, we were known as Rose Morgan and Joe Louis. He understood that I was a well-known businesswoman. He had no problem with me keeping my maiden name. He definitely had no ego."

The matchup between Louis and Primo Carnera on June 25, 1935, brought out fifteen thousand blacks to Yankee Stadium. Louis's prominent Harlem friends who were there to cheer him on included Adam Clayton Powell Jr., NAACP officials Roy Wilkins and Walter White, Harlem Hospital surgeon Louis T. Wright, Duke Ellington, Billy Rowe, and Billy Eckstine. Louis had twenty-two matches under his belt with no losses. He knocked out Carnera in the sixth round. That same year, Harlemites were rejoicing again when he quickly outpointed Max Baer in Yankee Stadium.

Joe Louis's string of victories came to an end in 1936 when he was knocked out by the German Max Schmeling in the twelfth round. Louis's eyes were swollen and bloody, his hands were swollen, and his fingers were sprained. His worried wife, Marva Trotter, was waiting in the Hotel Theresa for what was to be a celebration. "I don't care what you heard about me being modest, I wasn't," Joe said after the loss. "I was just as vain as Muhammad Ali. I just had to be more discreet about it. No way I was going to the Hotel Theresa that night looking the way I did. I didn't want my wife looking at me or all those black folk who had so much faith in me."

Blacks in Harlem took Joe Louis's loss to Max Schmeling personally. A number of them said that Louis lost the fight because he'd been drugged by his opponents. Another story that floated around Harlem was that Schmeling had iron in his gloves. After the loss, a humiliated Joe Louis said he wanted to get his hands on Schmeling again so badly he could taste victory.

Schmeling agreed to meet Joe Louis again in the ring at Yankee Stadium on June 22, 1938. In an ironic way, the fight was a forecast of World War II. It was viewed as Germany versus America. Max Schmeling was Hitler's exemplar of Aryan supremacy. For that reason, the burden of defending American democratic values fell on the shoulders of a lone black man. "Joe, we're depending on those muscles for America," said President Franklin Roosevelt. Even whites in the South who placidly endorsed yellowbellies with lynch ropes were pulling for the twenty-four-year-old black man. When Louis decked Schmeling in less than one minute after the bell rang for round one, "it was the shortest, sweetest minute of the entire thirties," said civil rights leader Roy Wilkins. Louis debunked Hitler's myth of Aryan supremacy. America's faith in Louis had been well placed. The entire nation was elated. Black Americans relished the victory as their own. After knocking Hitler's man off his Aryan pedestal, Joe Louis was undisputedly the most celebrated figure in the world in the late 1930s.

Prior to the match, Joe Louis and Max Schmeling posed for pictures. "Max and I were talking about things I'd read about the Aryan race being the only pure race," said Joe Louis. "Shoot! Max told me he never said those things and wouldn't think them. I believed him because he's been my friend since then; we stay, even to this day, in touch with one another. He looked at fighting the way I did. It was just a contest to see who's the strongest, the cleverest, the luckiest, and the best trained."

After Joe Louis's near instant disposal of Schmeling in their second match, thousands of blacks in Harlem and in cities around the nation took to the streets marching all night. "The people in Harlem went wild," said Joe Louis, "throwing bottles, tin cans, and cups from rooftops—they had to use tear gas to stop the rioting. Black people all over the country were out in the streets, celebrating for me. I felt good about the partying, but bad that people would go so crazy over my victory that they'd get into trouble with the police. . . . I know now this was the top of my career. I had the championship, and I had beaten the man who had humiliated me. America was proud of me, my people were proud of me, and since the fight, race relations were lightening up—who the hell could ask for more?"

After Louis's victory over Schmeling, he went to a big party at the Hotel Theresa. He had rented the second floor for the victory party. All the sporting types showed up from Detroit and Chicago. Billy Daniels, who was performing at Smalls' Paradise, dropped in and sang a few songs during the celebration.

"There was a time in the ring," wrote Billy Rowe, "when a Joe Louis victory meant swelling muscles, on thrust chests and inflated egos for beige Americans. And a Joe Louis victory called forth carnival time in Harlem. The dance halls were happy with ecstatic feet, the ginmills thronged with folks celebrating as though a new baby had been born into the family or Dad had earned a raise. The churches buzzed with the prayer of Thanksgiving. There were the ugly times, too. When Joe Louis lost and Harlem went to the cleaners . . . when some beige Big Towner turned ugly and brooding—turned upon their white neighbors within the community seeking a kind of empty, bitter, foolish revenge. The bad times were rare. The happy times were often."

Just like when Joe fought Billy Conn in 1941—Harlem and the Hotel Theresa turned into carnival atmospheres. "Traffic was tied up in Harlem again last night," reported the *New York Times* the day after the match. "Robert Leftridge, forty-seven, a Negro . . . suffered a leg injury attributed by the police to skylarking in the lobby of the Hotel Theresa." And when the champ outpointed Jersey Joe Walcott in 1948, the *Times* reported that Louis "had to fight his way through thousands of partisans to enter his victory headquarters at the Hotel Theresa."

With the Schmeling victory still fresh in their minds, white policemen made no arrests. Fred R. Moore, the old-fashioned aristocratic editor of the *New York Age,* was embarrassed by the boorish behavior of his race. He wrote, "Joe Louis not only represents his race, but as world champion, represents the United States. . . . Those of his race can harm him with their over enthusiasm."

Louis was a shining star, and black Americans, excessively and constantly, lavished him with praise. In his modest way, he easily accepted their need to make a big deal over his success.

June 19, 1946, was declared Joe Louis Day in Harlem, which meant a parade on Seventh Avenue. Carl Lawrence, president of

Harlem NAACP branch, worked around the clock to make the day special for Joe and his fans. The Hotel Theresa, "the glamour castle," was booked with celebrities, high rollers, big-moneyed gamblers, showgirls from across the nation, and a number from the Continent here for the big day. There was talk in the hotel bar that a number of folks were planning to sleep in Central Park. Among those who planned to extend their trip beyond the parade for Louis's match with Billy Conn, scheduled for August, were Marian Anderson, Duke Ellington, and Claude Hopkins.

Although Joe Louis was socially clumsy and inarticulate, he was irresistibly good-looking and charming. "He is magnetic and disturbing," a Harlem society writer told her female readers. "He upsets your apple cart of what the socially trained gentleman should do. But you like it. . . . Joe Louis gets in your hair." The regulars at the Theresa bar knew when Joe Louis was in town because the big-moneyed gamblers—the sporting types—always followed him. Filing into the bar, these professional gamblers came from St. Louis, Los Angeles, Chicago, Kansas City. And Louis's collection of pretty black groupies crammed into the bar and spilled out into the lobby and onto Seventh Avenue. His famous dalliances became an amusing sport for the reporters and regulars seated at the bar, who invariably placed bets on which girls Joe Louis would choose for his group of companions for the night.

If the Theresa's walls could speak, we would probably know more about Joe Louis's sex life than our ears could bear. These stories about the champ are plentiful, sordid, and often funny.

His paramours in the hotel and around Harlem included showgirls, musicians, waitresses, actresses, cigarette girls, housewives, clerks, barmaids, and society women of both races. "It was widely known around the hotel and throughout Harlem that the champ enjoyed multiple sex partners," recalled a longtime Harlem resident. There were the dancers Ruby Dallas Allen and Edna Mae Holly, actresses Mildred "Acquanetta" Davenport, Fredi Washington, Lana Turner, Sonja Henie, and Lena Horne. Joe Louis's "bad boy behavior" and his addiction to mainly light-skinned and petite black women kept his flunkies, Freddie Guinyard, Leonard Reed, and Sunnie Wilson, busy in the hotel.

Joe Louis's sidekicks took his companions in groups of four upstairs to his suites. Between groups, he'd recover, then send for the next group. These women were after more than sex. They wanted money from Louis. Some days, Louis doled out as much as $5,000.

"These ladies couldn't pay their rent," said a longtime Harlem resident. It was worth their time to squeeze into the bar and hang out in the lobby and wait for one of Joe's flunkies to come for them. It was known around the Theresa that Joe Louis was a sucker for a sad story. If you could get close to him, you'd get a nice piece of money.

"Many of the women who slept with Joe Louis suffered female problems. They had to see doctors," said a longtime Harlemite. "Joe was overly endowed. That's why men often said they didn't want a woman who had been with Joe Louis."

"Yes, I heard that Joe was rough in bed," said musician Michael Jameson. "I mean rough in the sense that women couldn't resist him."

"He was our meal ticket," said Sunnie Wilson. "We kept bad things from happening to him. We kept the scandals away. Gangsters, certain kind of women, people who might want to get him off into different directions."

Few of the old bar regulars could forget the story that circulated around Harlem about Joe Louis's well-publicized return from a European tour in 1943. The champ's usual collections of women were waiting for him in the Theresa lobby, while others waited in their apartments and in nightclubs around Harlem. The champ made his paramours happy by giving each of them a bottle of the same French perfume. To top the gifts, he whispered to each lady, "I brought this back just for you." To him, it was worth the $100 he paid the agent to get that amount of French perfume through customs.

The beautiful Cotton Club dancer Cleo Hayes was compared to Lena Horne. There were always comparisons about who was the most beautiful. Some said she was even prettier than Lena Horne. But she, like Horne, was also a Joe Louis love interest.

"I knew I had a big appetite," admitted Joe Louis. "It's like I like steak, lamb chops, chicken, apples, and bananas. I like each at different times, but I have to have them all. It was a bad period. I was going through something like what happens to an alcoholic when he falls off the wagon. I got drunk with all these beautiful exciting women."

Joe Louis's temper was revealed in an ugly scene in the hotel lobby one night. A number of people in the hotel were surprised to see that side of Louis. A young woman was planning to attend a movie with Louis, Edna Mae Holly, and Sugar Ray Robinson. The young lady was dressed to the nines. She was planning to be Joe's date for the evening.

"We were going to a John Wayne movie," recalled the woman,

now in her seventies. "I was a bit miffed because Joe had brought two women from Detroit and he said that I wasn't going with him to the movie. I put my hand on my hip and shook my finger in his face and said, 'I'm going with you.' We argued back and forth. He kept telling me that I wasn't going. He ordered me upstairs to my room. I stood there for a minute or so. Then he slapped me so hard that tears began to roll down my face. It seemed as though everybody in the lobby was looking at me. I ran to the elevator and went up to my room.

"Marva [Joe Louis's wife] didn't always come to New York with him. She only came with him when there was a fight or some other event. But he always came with his entourage. And there were always girls waiting for him in New York. [Sugar] Ray lived in New York but he was at the Theresa often. He was a bit more discreet than Joe about his affairs. Plus, Edna Mae kept a pretty tight rein on him. But he'd cut loose from her and slip out with Joe and others from time to time. Although Ray and Edna Mae no longer lived in the hotel, Ray would stay there quite often. He always stayed in the Theresa when he had a fight in New York."

"Joe's henchmen weren't able to keep his reputation with women from the NAACP," recalled Judge James Watson. Joe was into women and everybody in the Theresa and everybody in Harlem knew it. Billy Rowe had a letter-writing campaign begun in early 1940s nominating Joe Louis for black America's most prestigious award, the NAACP's Spingarn Medal. This coveted award is given out annually to an American of African descent. After all, Joe Louis was the heavyweight champion and the most revered black man in the world. He was a major contributor to the NAACP. Louis was friendly with Walter White, the NAACP's most senior administrator. The NAACP had nothing against giving the medal to sports figures, because Jackie Robinson and Hank Aaron would be recipients of the medal in later years.

By 1945 when Joe Louis had become an international celebrity, notables who had received the award included W. E. B. Du Bois, Mary McLeod Bethune, A. Philip Randolph, Charles Drew, and Walter White. But the gentlemen and gentlewomen who prided themselves on being part of that noble class the talented tenth could never bring themselves to award Joe Louis the most prestigious medal that his race offered. None of this went over well with Joe's fans in Harlem and those in the Theresa. "I have often wondered just why our top Negroes, and I mean in this instance those in leadership brackets, have persisted in a hands-off snooty attitude toward Joe Louis, the number one figure among Negroes today," argued columnist Dan Burley. "I think it is high time that we stop being hincty in the way we regard one another and the sooner we learn that there is no such thing as an exclusive Negro and that we are all in the same boat, the better it is going to be for everybody."

Joe Louis was, however, conspicuously absent from Walter White's famous parties in his Sugar Hill apartment that was dubbed "the White House." The Walter Whites entertained such intellectuals and artists of both races as Ira Gershwin, Fannie Hurst, Roy Wilkins, Herbert Lehman, Langston Hughes, Ralph Bunche, and the famous Harlem surgeon Louis T. Wright.

Eight

BILL BROWN'S DEBUT
(1948–58)

The Hotel Theresa that Walter Scott envisioned when he became manager in 1940 was a place for the better element of the race—certain entertainers, the professionals, the successful businesspeople, the eminent achievers, and others of unblemished social, moral, and ethical background. Scott's vision didn't become a reality, but he had worked hard to maintain the Hotel Theresa as a respectable establishment. "Gertrude Scott told me that her husband [Walter Scott] was ill," recalled Scott family friend Hazel Ferebee. "That was in 1947. His job at the Theresa had become very stressful, and he was advised by his doctor to resign. Their daughter, Gladys, had finished college at New York University. I think she had married then. She married Robert Mangum, who eventually became a deputy police commissioner in New York. After Walter Scott resigned from the hotel, the family moved into the new Riverton Apartments on East 135th Street."

In the fall of 1948, Thomas Cooke of the Gresham Management Company put out a press release announcing the new management team for the Hotel Theresa. William (Bill) Harmon Brown was named resident manager. Brown had actually begun his duties as manager in the spring of 1948. His immediate staff included his

Bill Brown. *Photograph by Cecil Layne. Courtesy of Cecil Layne.*

assistant manager, Frank Hailstolk, and Felix Graves, manager of food services.

"There was a world of difference between Walter Scott and Bill Brown," recalled Naidine Collins. "Walter Scott had high standards and didn't believe in nonsense. Bill Brown was a player. One minute he could act like a professional around the hotel—meeting and welcoming all the big shots who came. He could exhibit charm and personality and class. Then he'd hit on the girls around the hotel or put gambling games together. That man was addicted to gambling. Walter Scott would have never permitted gambling in the Theresa. They were like night and day. Bill had a temper at times too."

The son of a minister, Bill Brown was raised in a traditional family. He was born on January 31, 1916, to Nancy Nickens Brown and

Gilbert Brown Jr. in a small town aptly named Steelton, Pennsylvania. The Pennsylvania Steel Company plant was founded there in 1867. Situated alongside the Susquehanna River, Steelton borders on Harrisburg.

Bill entered Howard University in 1935. As an honor student, he earned a National Youth Administration scholarship, which was funded by a New Deal program for students who had earned at least a B average. He joined the popular Omega Psi Phi fraternity and enjoyed the usual parties with his fraternity brothers on campus.

"Bill was my classmate at Howard University," recalled longtime friend Hazel Ferebee. "He was always outgoing and a popular basketball player while in college. He was tall, handsome, and full of charisma and personality. His best friend was another basketball player. His name is Willie Wynn. The last time I saw him [Willie Wynn], he was living in Brooklyn. The two were always together on campus. The girls loved Bill back then. He didn't have to come on to them, they came on to him. In college, Bill was always elegantly dressed. Years later, when I came to know Bill again at the Theresa, that never changed—he was still impeccably groomed at all times. I knew his girlfriend Gloria Osborne. She was a classmate at Howard. She came from a proper Washington family. I think she had relatives connected with the university."

After graduating from Howard in the class of 1939, the charismatic Brown landed a plum job with the Federal Housing and Home Financing Administration, now called the Department of Housing and Urban Development. He was among the first of his race to work in a professional capacity in the agency. His responsibilities included placing poor families in low-income housing.

Bill Brown married Gloria Osborne on July 17, 1940, in Washington. The Osbornes liked Bill Brown, but they thought Gloria was too young to marry. She was eighteen years old and had completed just one year of college.

"When my uncle first brought her [Gloria] to Harrisburg, I used to follow her around," recalled Bill's nephew Nick Jones. "She was so beautiful. Her family in Washington was well connected. Her father was a civil servant, but he knew all the gangsters and big numbers guys across the nation. It was that era, you know. Her father helped Bill get the job with the Federal Housing and Home Financing Administration. People were impressed by money no matter how you made it. Gangsters had connections with the police, judges, lawyers, and the best people. It was the way things were in those days."

"Gloria was always a lovable person, a sweet person," said fellow high school classmate Edward Brooke. "She was very popular, but very quiet. Not an aggressive person by any means."

Bill and Gloria's only child, Ronald (Ronnie) Harmon Brown, was born on August 1, 1941, in Washington. In 1942, the Federal Housing agency transferred Bill to Boston. Five years later, he was sent to the agency's New York office.

After six months in New York, the Gresham corporation hired him. "It was my uncle's background in housing that got him the job at the hotel," said Nick Jones. Brown had a natural flair for public relations and he had personality galore—attributes that his predecessor lacked. He produced more stories for the press on the hotel in his first few months than Walter Scott had generated in his eight-year tenure.

The Browns' twelfth-floor penthouse suite was tastefully decorated with classic English furniture. "There was a long, rectangular fish tank filled with fishes," recalled Nick Jones. "You couldn't miss it when you walked into their suite. It was near the entranceway."

The three-bedroom suite's large formal living and dining rooms were sufficient for the lavish Sunday-evening cocktail parties Gloria and Bill threw for Harlem notables like Langston Hughes, the Lionel Hamptons, Adam Clayton Powell Jr., Duke Ellington, Thurgood Marshall, Paul Robeson, and an assortment of Harlem's best-known people. During these evenings, guests had lively and spirited conversations about contemporary and social issues. Bill Brown included his young son, Ronnie, in his social world. Ronnie was seven when the Browns moved into the Theresa. He would live in the hotel for nearly ten years. It was no wonder that the child would grow up to head the National Democratic Party and serve as a secretary of commerce under Bill Clinton (1993–1996).

The writer Stephen Holmes gave an example of young Ronnie's precocious behavior during one of the Browns' Sunday gatherings. Family friend Martha Lewis was making an obvious play for a handsome bachelor. Lewis, trying to maintain a bit of dignity, began a seductive prance and a series of "subtle winks" in full view of her quarry. Lewis thought only the gentleman she was trying to entice noticed her flirting. She was mistaken. Ronnie said, "Martha, you should buy yourself some overalls." Surprised that Ronnie had witnessed her mating call, she asked, "What do you mean?" "Because you're working so hard," the youngster responded. Had Bill Brown heard his son's response, he would have let out a deep belly laugh and given Ronnie his highest approval.

In the early 1950s, talk at the Browns' cocktail parties and throughout the hotel centered on the fate of black Americans, which rested on the shoulders of Thurgood Marshall. The NAACP's top lawyer was spending considerable time in the NAACP offices in consultation with his brilliant team of lawyers, historians, and educators setting the strategy and calling the plays for the impending showdown with the Supreme Court. The 1954 *Brown* Supreme Court decision struck down for public education the "separate but equal" doctrine of *Plessy vs. Ferguson.* The NAACP victory didn't abolish legal segregation in restaurants, hotels, and parks, but it did send forth a signal. A few hotels downtown saw the writing on the wall and began discreetly permitting black patronage. In the mid-1950s, downtown hotels began chipping away at the Theresa's clientele.

One of Bill Brown's first major tasks as manager was to oversee the hotel's extensive renovations, which had to be ready in time for the Joe Louis–Jersey Joe Walcott fight. The renovations had started under Walter Scott. But Bill anticipated that reporters would use lots of ink to write about the happenings of the beautiful people who graced the halls of the Theresa, and there would be stories on the new "innkeeper," as he liked to call himself.

In June 1948, within a couple of weeks of Bill Brown's becoming manager, the Joe Louis–Jersey Joe Walcott fight took place. Brown turned away guests in droves because former manager Walter Scott had booked all three hundred rooms. Without naming Bill Brown, Billy Rowe took a swipe at the new manager in a July 1948 column: "There had been chaos loosed on the Theresa by the latest Louis fight." Rowe didn't think that Brown understood the way things worked in the hotel—mainly, how rooms got assigned. "Many of the reservations honored by existing manager Walter Scott were ignored by the new chief of staff, and some of the big shots found their rooms occupied by small fries."

Rowe might have been thinking about A. G. Gaston, who was turned away from the Theresa during this time. An Alabama native and Booker T. Washington disciple, A. G. Gaston had amassed a fortune in the funeral home and insurance businesses in the segregated South by the early 1940s. Gaston was famous for telling black people they could become empowered by seeking "green power." When he arrived at the Theresa for the Louis–Walcott fight, Gaston was taken aback because even the cleaning people in the hotel weren't impressed by him.

"I spotted Mr. Gaston at the desk," recalled hotel messenger Horace Carter. "He was yelling and complaining about wanting a room. Nobody else had recognized him, it seemed. He was not happy about being treated like an ordinary person. I went up to him and introduced myself and he explained that there were no rooms available. I called Bill Brown to let him know that Mr. Gaston was in the lobby trying to get a room. Mr. Gaston was the richest black man in Alabama. I thought Bill would let him have a room. Maybe Bill was just exhausted or something. But A. G. Gaston was turned away. So I walked him to the Braddock Hotel, where they were happy to have him."

The hotel's publicity director released a statement that announced the new modernization of the Theresa. New manager, Bill Brown, delighted in showing off the new amenities in time for a Joe Louis main event. The new manager stated that, "With the recent

Louis–Walcott fight bringing thousands of people to New York from all over the country—hundreds of Negro guests jamming the Hotel Theresa had a chance to witness the management's $100,000 modernization program at first hand." The release pointed out the new renovations that were nearing completion. A number of new conveniences and added services such as a new bar and cocktail lounge were added. A private dining room for special events was opened. An air conditioning system was set up in the new facilities. The hotel installed video equipment which claimed to be the most modern and the largest hotel television connection of its kind in the nation. In order to give all guests more efficient service, the facilities opened for longer hours. A new soda fountain was added to provide guests of the hotel with a variety of tasty and popular refreshments that were moderately priced.

Early in his tenure as manager, Brown cultivated a personable relationship with the black press. He made sure his bartenders gave them tips about hotel celebrity guests and free drinks. As part of the hotel's renovations, the pressroom on the second floor was upgraded with new comfortable furnishings and office equipment. The new manager welcomed all the whoop-de-do in his hotel that celebrated Louis's victory. He relished the excitement; Brown was in his element. "Bill Brown, in the manager's post at the Theresa, will be figuring out how he can keep the wolves out of the lobby," wrote Billy Rowe. During the festivities that followed the fight, Brown was introduced to the heavy betters from across the nation. The regulars were on hand, such as Bumpy Johnson, the Ross brothers, Bill "Bojangles" Robinson, and Finley Hoskins. They would become fixtures at Bill Brown's notorious gambling games in the hotel.

Rowe was thinking about the heavy betters when he told his

readers, "The Joe Louis–Jersey Joe Walcott cuffyclacth isn't the only thing the smart money makers are betting on. The latest wager along hustler's row is 3 to 1 that this country and Russia will stay out of open war the rest of the year. There are no such hopes for '49, however, and you can expect the draft to go into full motion by fall after the final vote comes out of Congress this summer."

Following Joe Louis's victory over Walcott, high-spirited enthusiasts typically became incorrigible, causing near-riot conditions to erupt in the lobby and spill out to Seventh Avenue. There were those at the bar who had had too much to drink. The reefer-puffing crowd were loud in their jubilance. The heroin addicts forgot where they were staying. A number left their motors running and created traffic jams on Seventh Avenue all night.

According to Martha Lewis, a Brown family friend, "Bill had a lot of charisma. He could engage anyone in conversation, whether they were sports figures, newspaper people, musicians, writers, or political figures. He was comfortable with everybody. I think being exposed to that had a great deal of influence on Ron, 'cause Ron certainly had his father's charisma."

"Oh, Bill Brown was wonderful," said family friend Hazel Thomas. He was lots of fun, an all-around smart guy with a wonderful personality. He was cut out for a job like that."

"My grandfather loved that job," said Bill Brown's grandson Michael Brown. "He was the man. When you're manager of the only good hotel that takes black people and has a wonderful bar and a great restaurant, you're somebody people want to know."

"He [Ronnie] left Harlem every weekday morning and ventured

into the virtually all-white world of his exclusive West Side prep school, where he knew he was expected to interact with his classmates and with everyone he met in a manner that would not reflect negatively on his family or his race," said the writer Stephen Holmes. "Then he came home to the fabled capital of Negro America. Bill and Gloria's decisions about the best school for their son required him to lead a racially schizophrenic existence."

Ronnie's parents let him roam freely around the hotel after school and on weekends. He'd help the bellhops by running around to Seventh Avenue to flag cabs, for guests, assist the waitresses by clearing away dishes, or work with the bartenders when they unloaded merchandise. He had fun playing with the old-fashioned hand-operated elevator, which he would playfully operate while nervous hotel guests looked on.

Vice President Richard Nixon came to the Theresa in 1952. Nixon was visiting Harlem to drum up support in the black community for the Republican Party. Nixon and his wife, Pat, greeted various Harlem politicians and dignitaries in the Theresa. Eisenhower and Nixon received over 30 percent of the black vote in the 1952 election. Bill Brown made sure that his young son got to meet the vice president. Years later, Ron Brown noted that meeting Nixon at the hotel in his early life convinced him to be a Democrat.

"My father's childhood friends were always eager to visit him at the famous Theresa Hotel," said Tracey Brown, Ron Brown's daughter. "Dad would lead them through the lobby and public areas, but eventually they'd end up on the roof to play Dad's favorite game: filling balloons with water and dropping them on the pedestrians below. When my grandparents found out, they made my father understand that he could unintentionally hurt someone, a baby in a carriage, for example, and he stopped."

"He [Ronnie] was a child, and he was really trying to help the staff in the hotel," recalled waitress Debbie McDade. "We'd put up with him because he was the boss's kid." Relief struck the hotel workers when the youngster headed to his favorite place, the hotel's rooftop. He'd spend hours romping with his Doberman.

"What an active little boy he was!" says Hazel Thomas Gray, a New Yorker who staged charity affairs in the hotel. "The Browns had an apartment in the Theresa, and we would drop by and see them. When he could get out of the apartment, he'd go skithering down the hall, and they'd call after him, 'Don't go in there! Ronnie, don't go in there!'"

"Dad was intrepid," wrote Tracey Brown. "When the great Ray Charles was going through a heroin withdrawal, GD [Bill Brown] and Cousin Bobby slipped him into the hotel through a back entrance and took him in the freight elevator up to his room. My father, thirteen, popped into the elevator and asked for an autograph from the singer, who was near collapse and literally foaming at the mouth. When Bobby said, 'Ronnie, this is not the time,' Dad withdrew."

"My earliest years were spent walking the lobbies and the hallways and the dining rooms," Ron Brown would later recall. "I was able to absorb the sights and sounds and mysteries. I was able to watch and learn from the great African-American cultural and political leaders and the great athletes who made their way to Harlem."

"To hear him [Ron Brown] talk about it, his parents ran Harlem," said Michael Brown. "Growing up in the Theresa, surrounded by all those role models—Joe Louis, Roy Campanella, Paul Robeson, Jackie Robinson—that's how my dad got a lot of his foundation, his nurturing. He had a sense of how people got things done.

"My dad would have Joe Louis sign six or seven pieces of paper. Louis would say, 'Why do you need all of these, Little Brown?' 'I just like 'em, I like to paste 'em all over my room.' But what my dad was doing was keeping one for himself and selling the rest at school. Louis found out about it and said, 'That's it, Little Brown. No more autographs for you.' "

"I always knew when Joe Louis was in town," recalled Evelyn Cunningham. "Ronnie Brown would tell me. He was a good source. He understood what I did. And we remained friends until he died."

"Being exposed to all kinds of people in the hotel—the celebrities, the sports folks—made him more sophisticated than his peers. That within itself was a tremendous education. Nothing after that experience came as a shock to him," recalled Nick Jones. "He had seen it all before he left the hotel as a teenager."

"Dad spent a lot of time with his friend Billy Perry, alternating between looking for girls in Billy's home community of St. Albans, Queens, and seeking more sophisticated pursuits at the Hotel Theresa and its environs," said Tracey Brown. "Sometimes they'd start on Friday night and end on Saturday morning. Even though my father was a lightweight drinker—one or two drinks was his limit— he was a serious partygoer. The scene at the Theresa during Dad's last year of high school was, as Billy recalled, 'party time.' You wonder how Ronnie got any studying done there."

"Life in the Theresa made him confident," said Ron Brown's childhood friend and New York surgeon John Nailor. "He believed that he could do anything. It made him a lot more sophisticated at an earlier age. He matured quicker. He developed a tenacity to his personality. It came out of the Hotel Theresa environment. It was definitely that unique experience of growing up in the Theresa. To grow up in the center of black existence had to have an impact on his life—but in the most positive ways. As Ron grew older, graduated from college, joined the military, and went to Korea, Bill was very proud of his son. He always ran around bragging about him. He was definitely in Ron's corner."

"The singer Dinah Washington lived in the penthouse suite across from the Browns, where she hosted loud, wild parties in her place," recalled Marjorie Corbitt. "Popular Harlem emcee Pee Wee Marquette frequented Dinah's parties. They'd be up all night partying. Some weird stuff was going on there. There was a popular Harlem transvestite who'd be there. He worked at one of the clubs. They'd sit on each other's laps. Nobody knew what any of that was about. Dinah was rowdy. She abused all of her husbands. She took lots of pills and drank a whole lot."

"She [Dinah] talked all bad," said famed radio personality Hal Jackson. "But she had a tender heart." Dinah couldn't resist pampering the boss's son. She kept Ronnie's cookie jar filled with cookies that she baked especially for him.

By 1948 the winds of the World War II had blown over America, and the elegant ballroom that Walter Scott had only dreamed of became a reality under Bill Brown's management. On August 17, 1948, Bill Brown put out a press release that read, "An outstanding, completely new surprise package will soon be unwrapped when the grand ballroom is finished. For the first time in Harlem's history, or anywhere else in America, there will be a hotel catering to colored people with a spacious, sumptuous large capacity ballroom right in the Theresa Hotel." Dan Burley gave some added publicity to the hotel's new ballroom when he wrote, "Theresa Hotel manager Bill Brown was working hard on plans for the opening of the hotel roof as a ballroom." The following New Year's Eve, Bill Brown showed off the lavish new Skyline Ballroom. At night, from its tall, elegantly dressed windows, the scintillating scene was breathtaking. The illuminated arches of the George Washington Bridge were north, the glittering lights of the Triborough Bridge were east, and the south view held the splendor of the Empire State Building.

"At that time there were so many social clubs, I mean, so many of them," said singer Juanita Howard. "There were those you might consider the elites and those at another level like the Elks, the Ma-

Diahann Carroll with other beauty contestants in the Hotel Theresa, 1950s. *Courtesy of Ophelia DeVore.*

sons, the Order of the Eastern Star, the 149th Street Association of North Carolina. So many had these clubs and they would give these dances all over the place. The Skyline Ballroom was very busy."

"There was a lot of Negro profiling going on at the Theresa," recalled Preston Wilcox. "You had to be of a certain class to get into the Skyline Ballroom." A number of Harlemites accepted the Skyline as a place for the NAACP and Urban League types. They understood that Bill Brown didn't permit the nonprofessional class to host their wedding or other events there.

"If you had a wedding in the Skyline Ballroom," recalled Ron Brown years after he left the hotel, "you had to be top-shelf."

When it came to the guest list for the private parties the Browns hosted in their penthouse, or the patrons who would gather in the Skyline Ballroom, the new centerpiece of the hotel, then class mattered to Bill Brown.

"Black people preferred being at the Theresa. There was a psychological security for celebrities and others being in Harlem," said Horace Carter. "I think of it now as a Mecca. I say that because everything that was important to Harlemites and to African-Americans happened in the Theresa—the rallies outside, the political meetings inside, the cotillions, the weddings, and business meetings. Especially after the Skyline Ballroom opened, the hotel could accommodate every aspect of our race's needs and desires."

Bill Brown added the special Easter dinner to the dining room's menu. The orchid room now offered roast Easter lamb au jus with mint jelly, one-half spring chicken, butter carrots, chiffonade salad, roasted sugar-cured ham with glazed pineapple. Dinner including an appetizer was $2.25 per person in the early 1950s.

"There's no excuse for being an ordinary Negro," Bill Brown often said. His friends described him as good-natured and generous to a fault, but he relished living on the edge—courting danger. On the other hand, his wife, Gloria, the former debutante, found the all-night poker games with the hotel's fast crowd distasteful.

"His overexuberance in money matters became a serious problem," said John Nailor. "He had a big ego," remembered family friend George Lopez. "He liked to put on a show—whether he could afford it or not."

Bill made no effort to keep his designs on pretty women discreet. By all accounts, Bill and Gloria were seemingly ill-suited. "Gloria acted like Pat Nixon to me. Kind of timid-acting like Pat Nixon," recalled Debbie McDade. "I'd see her often because the family ate breakfast at the counter almost every morning."

It appeared to a number in the hotel that Bill was simply being a courteous innkeeper offering hospitality when he paid what seemed to be more than the usual attentiveness to pretty young female guests. They were his dates in the hotel dining room or at the bar, which meant he picked up the tab for expensive wines and steak dinners. His appetite got even bigger after midnight when he used his pass key to enter their rooms for his nightly pleasures.

"There were certain females in the hotel who fell behind in their rent," recalled Naidine Collins. "If Bill had something going on with them, they could stay until he lost interest. That meant another female excited him more. When that happened, the female who had fallen out of favor had to go. It didn't matter to him that she sometimes had no place to go. He simply moved on to the next pretty face."

A prim and proper registered nurse who lived in the Theresa recalled a late-night surprise encounter with the philandering manager. "Bill Brown, talk about a cad! That ain't the word," she said. "I can't find a word in the dictionary to describe him. One night shortly after I was married, my husband and I were getting ready for bed. We heard a key in our lock. My husband jumped up and opened the door. It was Bill Brown standing there. My husband asked him what was he doing at our door. And I quickly told him that we were married. I didn't want him assuming that I was shacking up or that kind of thing. He said he didn't know that I had gotten married. Then he asked if he could stay anyhow. My husband told him to get out."

"Bill Brown would have slept with a gnat if he could have kept it down," said Naidine Collins. "But he wouldn't have even thought about going into Anna Arnold Hedgeman's or Grace Nail Johnson's suites. They would have had him fired!"

"Bill wasn't shy at all about what he wanted," said a Harlemite who knew Bill Brown. "He'd walk up to you and say, 'Hey there, you got some big breasts there.' He didn't have to know you to say such outlandish, disrespectful things."

"Yeah, Bill liked the girls, all right," said Judge James Watson.

His behavior toward women left some people confused. "Gloria was such a beautiful woman," said Dessie Harper, a friend of the Brown family's. "We wondered why he had to be such a womanizer." "He was a party guy," said Evelyn Cunningham. "He was very attracted to women, and women were very attracted to him."

"Bill Brown," Mary Louise Williams recalled, "reminded me of Bill Clinton. He had a magnetic personality. He didn't always pursue women, they came on to him. That's how I saw it. But he was a good manager of the hotel."

"There were always women around," recalled John Nailor.

"There was no attempt to hide being a womanizer. Women were very available in that house."

"You have to realize no matter how gross Bill Brown's behavior was, he was educated and was accepted as a member of the black elite. He definitely saw himself as a member of that class," recalled a hotel resident. "He would play around with chorus girls and barmaids, but he wasn't going to have one of them as his wife. They certainly weren't going to be invited to the parties in his home or in the Skyline Ballroom."

"Bill Brown knew exactly which women in the hotel were available," recalled Jewel Sims Okala. "He knew the kind of women who would permit his crude behavior. There were attractive ladies in the Theresa all the time—from schoolteachers to showgirls, all types. Ladies in the hotel didn't go into the bar. If a female went into the bar alone, she was saying, 'I'm available.' It was just that simple."

"Years after Bill Brown left the Theresa, a group of us from the city were on Fire Island attending a party," recalled a longtime Harlemite. "Bill chased me around the place. I was in my twenties and he had to be in his fifties. He did that in front of the other guests."

"Bill Brown ran a gambling room in the Theresa every Saturday night," recalled a fellow gambler who lived in the hotel. "You know he was shrewd, even a bit shady. Five or six gambling tables would be set up, and he'd cut the game—he'd take a percentage—like ten percent from each pot. Sometimes, we shared in the take. International gamblers like Finley Hoskins and Danny Sims were regulars in there. They were into shooting crap too. Danny Sims was a big-time pimp. He'd stop by the bar in the evenings to brag about how many whores he had. Sometimes if his [Bill's] old college buddies showed up—he called them the Howard alumni group—he'd let them join the game. Those games lasted all night."

"Bill had his own private cook for the gambling room," recalled Horace Carter. "None of the hotel employees were allowed in the room. It was strictly for high rollers. If I needed to speak to Bill about something, I'd call him on the telephone. Bojangles hung out there before he died. He would pistol-whip anyone's butt when he lost. His pistol had a white pearl handle. Would get his money back. That cat had a temper. He was mean when he lost. Nobody played around with him. But somehow he was called the unofficial mayor of Harlem. Never understood that."

"Everyone knew Bumpy, and he introduced me to the great black dancer Bill 'Bojangles' Robinson, whom Bumpy idolized," said Helen Lawrenson, "and who used to be a fast man in a fight himself, in his younger days. 'Man, he could really go,' Bumpy said. 'He solid laid it.' "

"One night there was some trouble in the gambling room," said one of the regular gamblers. "One of the hotheads in there threatened to kill Bill. Sometimes, Bill would try to get slick in the games. The cat was tall—way over six feet. The cat had his hands around Bill's neck and had his head hanging out of the window. Everybody thought Bill was a goner."

Naidine Collins offered another account of the episode. She said it was one of Bill's fellow gamblers who had his hands around the throat of the manager. "Some of the guys came running into the lobby saying the man was going to kill Bill Brown. The man was mad as hell. I assumed that Bill was cheating the men out of some money.

He had Bill's head hanging from the window while choking him. I thought he was going to kill Bill. One of the other men managed to get him off Bill."

"My husband and I went to the Theresa one night," recalled Hazel Ferebee. "His dental association was hosting a function there and he wanted to speak to Bill. We asked around and learned that Bill was in the gambling room. I told my husband, 'We're going straight up to the Skyline Ballroom. We're not going near Bill and all that gambling.' Walter Scott was an Alpha [Alpha Phi Alpha fraternity] man like my husband. Mr. Scott would have never considered such behavior. All that gambling was shameful."

To keep his hotel full, Bill Brown permitted gangsters like Bumpy Johnson and Finley Hoskins to rent rooms for their whores. As time passed, and more of the fast crowd frequented the hotel under Brown's management. But that notwithstanding, his associations with Harlem's upper class enabled him to maintain a semblance of respectability for the hotel, long after its golden era was over.

Bill Brown was comfortable in both worlds. He was the perfect host while entertaining Harlem's upper class. Still, he withstood the rough world of gangsters even while cheating in gambling games that he controlled.

"Bill Brown could get red-hot mad too," recalled Horace Carter. "You know Bill would let cats come to the hotel and bring their girlfriends. They were usually married, you know. They'd stay one or two nights. These cats ordered steaks and expensive wine and put it all on their hotel tabs. Then they'd slip out of the hotel without paying. Bill would get so damn angry. He'd send me to their homes and say, 'Give the summons to their wives.' He would get his money."

Bill Brown had a big heart. Sometimes he had a motive for helping others, or often it was genuine. In 1951, Bill Brown insisted on putting up twenty-one Jamaican citizens who had stopped over in New York on their way to Europe. They had been recent victims of a hurricane that had swept the islands and wrecked their homes. Brown solicited the help of the Blumstein family of the department store and Reginald Pierrepoint of the *Amsterdam News*. The Caribbean travelers were put up in the Theresa and given clothes from Blumstein's. A number of them were journeying to England to study, some to find work, and others to join family members and seek a better life.

There was a disagreement between Bill Brown and the hotel owners in 1956. He was fired. The family took up residence in White Plains, New York. They lived near the Gordon Parks family. Bill tried to make a living by entering various ventures. He was a bondsman for a while. Then he took up another venture: selling a line of women's hair products. He always had a gimmick to make a living. "He was the type of person who would get these grandiose ideas about what he wanted to do, whether or not he had the background for it," said George Lopez. "We'd hear of some deal Bill was doing and say, 'There goes Bill again.' "

Andy Kirk managed the hotel in 1956 and 1957. Kirk lived at 555 Edgecombe Avenue. He founded the popular eleven-member band, the Dark Clouds of Joy, in Dallas, Texas, in 1926. By 1936, the band was called Andy Kirk and the Clouds of Joy, and they were based in Kansas City. The band's first big hit, "Until the Real Thing Comes Along," came in 1936. By 1942, the Kirk band featured seventeen pieces. "I have always been a realist," said Andy Kirk. "I saw the end of that big band era just to give you an example, we use a good bit, a very good job in a club out in Los Angeles during the war. The end of the big band era came in the late 1940s. The club owner came to New York and he thought if he could get my band to come out there, it would revive the era. Now I took my son, my son was playing tenor and he came along in the Bach era. I had him with me. When we played and showed him off, he got all the write-ups because this was the era. I had a few tunes I had around him and he tied it up. Then I saw that things were coming to an end. So I got a job managing the Hotel Theresa."

Love B. Woods decided to sell one of his Harlem flophouses because the city wanted to tear it down to build an apartment building on the site of Seventh Avenue and 142nd Street. Woods sold the Woodside for eighty thousand dollars cash. He wanted to take over the Hotel Theresa and turn it into the "Waldorf of Harlem." Woods had been in the hotel business for a long time, but he was old and senile. Although he was making a pile of money on the Woodside, it was a cathouse. The Woodside was a cash cow for him. He bought the Hotel Theresa against the better judgment of most people who knew the ailing and fragile condition of Woods's health.

As a devout Jehovah Witness, Andy Kirk couldn't reconcile his religion with the responsibilities of managing the most popular and diversified place in Harlem. Kirk also wanted to devote more of his time to writing music.

"Andy Kirk didn't have the personality to manage the Theresa. That hotel required a manager who could deal with all sorts of people," said Judge James Watson. "Aside from Bill Brown's womanizing, he was a good manager."

After Andy Kirk fell ill, the Hotel Theresa owners asked Bill

Brown to return to his former position. He was delighted to return to the hotel. His business schemes had not materialized. He missed the hotel and the steady paycheck. Young Ron was now a junior at the Rhodes School. Back at the helm of the Theresa, Bill Brown couldn't resist his gambling parties, his womanizing—all the temptations were there for him to enjoy again. He did.

By January 1958, Gloria Brown could no longer tolerate Bill's life in the fast lane. She moved out of the Hotel Theresa. She accepted a job as a salesclerk for Steuben Glass, the upscale Fifth Avenue store. Steuben Glass had a Jim Crow hiring policy. Gloria believed that she had to present herself as white in order to service the upper-class whites who shopped there. This meant that her only son was not permitted to go near her workplace. "I think we all knew that she wasn't pure white," said Sally Walker, who was an executive for Steuben Glass at the time.

"The money for the gambling games wasn't as plentiful for Bill. The hired cook was gone," recalled Danny Moore. "Bill was frying chicken backs for the players."

By this time, Bill couldn't even convince a fellow black hotel owner from Detroit to stay in the Theresa. In 1958 *Jet* magazine reported that the black owner from Detroit was always griping because he couldn't get blacks to stay in his hotel for conventions and conferences. His hotel was shunned for white Detroit establishments. Still, when he came to New York, he wouldn't stay in the Theresa. He set himself up in one of the top white hotels in downtown Manhattan.

By the late 1950s, a number of Bill's upstanding year-round residents had moved into new apartments like Lenox Terrace and the Riverbend. "There were lots of empty rooms in the hotel when Bill finally moved out," recalled John Nailor. "I remember we moved down to the lower floors, leaving the penthouse. It was me, Ron, Bill, and his nephews, Bobby and Nick. But we partied before leaving the hotel one last time."

In 1959, the *New York Age* reported that the "Hotel Theresa, for years the proud queen of Negro hotels in America but today only a maudlin burlesque of her former greatness, was hauled into Supreme Court like a commoner."

When management demanded a rent hike for sixty of the hotel's permanent residents, the court battle ensued. Six months later, the hotel fired seven switchboard operators and installed pay phones.

Nine

MIXING IT UP
Politics, Gangsters, Celebrities, and Society (1948–58)

The Theresa Hotel's famous blue marquee on Seventh Avenue—the entry and exit point for the most famous and infamous ever, where taxis, Cadillacs, and limousines waited for the Theresa's famous guests—was a tourist attraction itself. On any given day, you could stand within view and see bands of musicians gathering under the marquee to board buses to take them to their next gig. They would often play while stepladder orators shouted their radical preachments over their jazz and blues music.

"We lost communication when we lost the Theresa," said Charles Kenyatta. He was a bodyguard for Malcolm X. "People used to come from Connecticut, Massachusetts, and New Jersey to hear the speeches. I occupied the corner on many weekends. So did Pork Chop Davis-Foreman, and Arthur Reid. There was Sister Lucille. We called her Little Firebrand 'cause she was filled with fire. We lost our cohesiveness. Nobody was going to listen to anything but strong black nationalist rhetoric. Yes, [Preston] Wilcox is correct, we were saying what some black people were scared to say. It was all pure and strong black nationalism. It had to be strong. Nobody was going to stand around to hear the NAACP talk about that pitiful integration.

They needed talk that would start them to thinking—they needed provocative thoughts."

Pork Chop Davis-Foreman had participated in virtually every Harlem boycott since the early 1930s. He attempted to build an economic base in Harlem. Davis-Foreman approached state agencies about Harlem running its own numbers game, but in a legitimate system. Since Harlem's illegal numbers rackets were generating hefty profits for white mobsters, he believed that it should benefit the black community, who were in dire economic straits. His plan didn't materialize though. He denounced black leaders who wouldn't confront white gangster-run businesses and racist Jewish merchants who controlled Harlem's businesses.

"Arthur Reid and James Lawson were Pork Chop's protégés," said Preston Wilcox. "They were key Garveyites . . . Harlem orators on the corner outside the hotel. Pork Chop would yell through that bullhorn. He seemed to enjoy ridiculing the white man. He mocked Walter White and Roy Wilkins, calling them Uncle Toms. He mimicked the NAACP leaders, particularly when they came to the hotel to speak. Pork Chop would tell his audience, 'See, *we* at the NAACP ain't like some of these radicals Negroes.'

"The black nationalists owned that corner. I was used to the Negro whisper. If you wanted to say something about the white man, you whispered it. But those Harlem orators stood in front of the Theresa Hotel for the whole world to hear them. No other politician had any say-so about who could have a spot on the speakers' corner except Adam Clayton Powell Jr."

"Davis was a self-taught man who was very well read," recalled Jewel Sims Okala. "I saw him almost daily. If he wasn't on the

stepladder outside the hotel preaching, he'd be talking with someone in the lobby trying to convince them to read what he was handing out. He always had stacks of papers. And he'd give me materials
to read—usually materials on the subject of Africa."

During the fall of 1948, Bill Brown's staff set up a conference
room on the second floor of the hotel for Ted Poston, who was then
working for the *New York Post*, to meet and have drinks with a number of the black newspersons, including Major Robinson, George
Schuyler, Billy Rowe, and Dan Burley. The meeting was about President Truman's earnestness in campaigning for passage of his civil
rights initiatives. There had been an open-air meeting in Harlem the
Saturday before the Tuesday presidential election in 1948. Thousands of black New Yorkers showed up. They waited for hours to see
and hear the president. Mr. Truman was presented a medal by a
greater New York Committee of Protestant black preachers. This
open-air meeting was to provide him with a sounding board to appeal to black voters. After the president's speech, the meeting with
the black press was held in the Theresa to determine what their im-
pressions were of the president's speech. The president and his staff
viewed the black press as a one-issue group. When the black press
gathered at the hotel to make sense of Truman's presentation, they
concluded that the president understood that they didn't believe
that he was doing enough for civil rights and things weren't pro-
gressing as fast as they should be. Nevertheless, Truman worked
hard to keep African-Americans from leaving the Democratic Party
for his rival, Henry Wallace, who was traveling around the country
with Paul Robeson talking to black and white audiences and lam-
basting Jim Crow. Truman had talked up his own ten-point civil

Paul Robeson, late 1940s.
Photograph by John W. Mosley.
Courtesy of the Charles L.
Blockson Afro-American
Collection, Temple University.

rights program, which included abolishing the poll tax, establishing a federal commission on civil rights, passing a federal antilynching law, and making the civil rights section of the Justice Department a full division.

When Nat King Cole, one of the Theresa's favorite sons, married Maria Ellington in 1948, the hotel was practically empty. All those who weren't invited went to Abyssinian Baptist Church to stand out-side to glimpse the famous groom and bride. Roosevelt Zanders, who sold numerous Cadillacs to the stars, gave the couple free limousine service for their wedding guests.

"I was in Abyssinian Baptist Church for the wedding," said Nai-dine Collins. "I knew Maria Ellington's sister, Charlotte. She used to come to the Theresa to visit me all the time. We were good friends. Of course, I knew Nat, too."

The following year, Paul Robeson held a press conference of the Civil Rights Congress in the Carver Room in the Theresa. Robeson informed the 150 reporters about the Ku Klux Klan and American Legion vigilantes who had stopped his Peekskill, New York, concert to benefit the Harlem chapter of the Civil Rights Congress. More than a thousand locals in Peekskill had thrown glass, bricks, clubs, stones, and waved knives at the workers who came to serve as ushers and set up chairs. Families were beaten by the Ku Klux Klan and by those who claimed to be Hitler's followers. Stacks of slabs were placed by the angry mob to prevent thousands from entering the concert area. The mob spewed their hateful sentiments at Robeson and those who came to hear him sing. "We're Hitler's boys!" "Lynch

Robeson!" "Every nigger bastard dies here tonight!" were the hateful sentiments expressed by the mob.

During the press conference, Robeson called on the Justice Department to investigate the Peekskill riot. Robeson said, "I'm going to sing wherever the people want me to sing. My people and I won't be frightened by crosses burning in Peekskill or anywhere else." Two weeks later, thousands gathered near the Theresa Hotel to hear Robeson and others speak about the outrage in Peekskill. He announced that his second concert in Peekskill would take place the following September.

In 1949, the hotel lost one of its regular guests when Bill "Bojangles" Robinson died. "He was the most graceful tap dancer of them all," said writer Albert Murray. His soft-shoe and tap routines have been imitated by other dancers. Just three years before, Bill Robinson had celebrated sixty years in show business at the largest gathering ever recorded on Broadway at the Zanzibar Club. "As a trouper and artist, he has no peers," said Billy Rowe. Robinson was praised for his originality, particularly the memorable "stair dance" scene in the film *The Little Colonel*. Despite his earnings, which were estimated at $6,600 a week in the late 1930s, he died like pauper. Extravagance and a gambling habit were the reasons given for his descent from riches to rags. The who's who of the entertainment world gathered at Abyssinian Baptist Church for his funeral, though. They jostled for seats in the church, where Nat King Cole, Count Basie, Duke Ellington, Eddie "Rochester" Anderson, Bill Brown, Don Newcombe, and Jackie Robinson were in attendance.

Over three thousand people filed past his casket in the Harlem Armory to say good-bye to the unofficial mayor of Harlem.

Hotel residents and the entertainment community suffered another loss the following year, in 1950. Comedian, filmmaker, and actor Eddie Green passed away. He had produced and starred in the comedy *Dress Rehearsal,* which became the first all-black film to run on television on NBC, in New York City in 1940. Green had also produced another movie, *Come Midnight,* which starred Jimmy Baskett and Amanda Randolph, in 1940. "It was just about four months ago that the guys who knew him best stood at the foot of the bed of Eddie Green on the tenth floor of the Theresa Hotel and spoke words of encouragement in regard to his health," Billy Rowe said soberly to his readers. "Their words were shallow and their emotions were deep because within their hearts, they knew that the funny man was running this way for the last time. Just a few days ago Eddie departed this life and his death added to the sadness of the world. He was last seen when he stopped over in New York en route to California from Puerto Rico. The sickness which robs a man of his living health had even then taken its toll. Notwithstanding, he gave the impression that he felt that all would be well once he reached the shores of the Golden Coast, the section of the country where he had sought and found fame and which he had therefore adopted. However, it was fitting that he should be there in the Theresa, high above Seventh Avenue, the street that knew him when. Perhaps, beautiful words could be knitted together about the emotion that he must have had as he gazed out the window on the busy thoroughfare, upon the people who were dwarfed in his eyesight by height as they twisted and turned and were swallowed up by a store, a restaurant, a theatre, a ginmill there to belch out again with their emotions held tight within their breasts. These were all familar turns to Eddie because he had taken them many a time on both failure and success. They cloaked his dreams and dusted his ideals, for not of this environment he grew into the great stature which found him beloved when the Grim Reaper snatched away his breath and stilled his heart. It is always great wonderment as to the proper manner in which those who are left behind should accept death. It is as factual as living, as inevitable as night and day, yet the shock is always new and as hurting as a toothache.

"Perhaps more fortunate than millions who make up this huddle of habitation on the planet world, Green was endowed by fate with a knack that enabled him to spend his life well and age by age, the bargains were many. A warm sensitive character, Eddie attacked life with passion that added an immortal twang to living."

At the time of Green's death, news had reached Harlem and other black communities across the nation that the disgraced actor and Theresa regular Rex Ingram was serving time in a Kansas prison. Ingram had taken a fifteen-year-old white girl across the Kansas state line for immoral purposes. The *Green Pastures* and *Cabin in the Sky* movie star was sentenced to eighteen months in prison. Due to heavy legal expenses, he lost his home in Warm Springs Canyon, California. Ingram never regained the level of popularity and success he'd once enjoyed. When Theresa sidewalk captain Maceo Birch traveled to Los Angeles shortly after Ingram was released from prison, he reported to Billy Rowe that Rex Ingram was on the stroll trying to gain a movie contract and renew contacts. Despite his prison record, he made a minor comeback. He played an Indian chief in *Ramar of the Jungle* in 1952 and appeared in *Anna Lucasta* in 1958 and *Elmer Gantry* in 1960.

By the late 1940s, Joe Louis's excessive spending caught up with him. His handing out fifty-dollar bills to hangers-on to buy sharkskin suits at Henry Lokos on Eighth Avenue, the large sums of cash he doled out to family and friends and to anyone who gave him a sucker's story, caused his financial downfall. If being broke wasn't enough, he owed the government thousands of dollars in back taxes. He was in desperate need of a purse.

Joe Louis's trainer commented on his situation: "There's a lot of fast living—hopping from one place to another—and there's a lot of people hanging around . . . living off him and leading him into a lot of temptation he probably wouldn't get into if he wasn't caught up in that fast living."

Grandiosity consumed Joe Louis when he announced that he was returning to the ring to fight a much younger Ezzard Charles in 1950. His close friends pleaded with him to go down in history with dignity. They believed that he would be regarded as the best heavyweight champion ever. Louis was now thirty-six, and Charles was twenty-nine. Since it was a matter of money, Billy Rowe knew that he could come up with a scheme for Joe Louis to make money, just as the Joe Louis Punch had been successful in its day. The Joe Louis restaurant failed because Joe himself gave away the profits. Louis was determined that he would show the world that he wasn't too old for the game that had made him a world-class celebrity. In the ring with Charles, Louis lost. After the fight, Joe Louis was so battered that Sugar Ray Robinson had to put his shoes on. Billy Rowe, the clever wordsmith, couldn't string together words to express his feel-

Joe Louis and Billy Rowe, 1940s. *Photograph by John W. Mosley. Courtesy of the Charles L. Blockson Afro-American Collection, Temple University.*

ings about his friend's embarrassing loss. Sadly, Billy Rowe turned his column over to the famous cartoonist E. Simms Campbell, who was Joe Louis's good friend. Campbell made a personal appeal to Joe Louis in the column when he wrote, "It was the same story everywhere one went. But the saddest sight of all was on the next day, the morning after, in front of the Hotel Theresa. Someone's brother told someone else's cousin who had a friend who kept company with a girl that was in the know that Joe Louis was upstairs in the Theresa. The word spread like wildfire and for hours the silent throngs stood in front of the Theresa, lined the sidewalks, crammed the doorway of the stores. All they wanted was a look at Joe. Somehow, a reporter felt, it wasn't an urge for a curious stare or even an opportunity to boast of having glimpsed Joe Louis in defeat. A voice in a reporter's heart told him that these people wanted him to see them . . . wanted him to know they were still his people.

"I don't mean that you are an old man, Joe. I mean that you just aren't as sharp as you used to be. The heart is there and the old brain is working smoothly, but the reflexes and the legs and muscles just won't repond as smoothly and as quickly and as keenly as they once did. No man living will ever wear your crown . . . but your dynasty is over."

Earl Brown of the *Amsterdam News* said it was sickening that a neophyte like Ezzard Charles gave Joe Louis such grief. Brown asked his readers to provide the proud champ with any necessary material assistance. The days were gone when Joe Louis had a pending showdown and victory was in the air, the high rollers were in town, the parties were planned, and his groupies were crowded into the lobby.

Outside the hotel on the famous corner, there were newspapers with a photograph of Joe Louis on the back cover. His face was swollen and distorted. "That's Joe Louis, Daddy," said a little girl. "I know dear," he said. "Joe Louis didn't win the fight, you know it,

Daddy," she added. He said, "Now we have another man. But I just love Joe Louis." Harlem was a morgue, said Billy Rowe. Even in defeat, Harlem still loved Joe. No matter that Ezzard Charles was declared the victor after fifteen rounds, Joe Louis was still the champion in the hearts of Harlemites. The grief over Joe's loss to Charles had no color line. All New Yorkers were touched by the fall of Joe Louis. Black America's greatest black hero to date had fallen. By now, four other Theresa regulars were playing professional baseball: Jackie Robinson, Roy Campanella, Don Newcombe, and Dan Bankhead. But they could never replace Joe Louis in the hearts and minds of Americans.

By 1954, a new face was on the scene in boxing. The Hotel Theresa was almost emptied on the last weekend in October of 1954 when the Brooklyn-born Floyd Patterson, the twenty-one-year-old light-heavyweight contender and outstanding American in the 1952 Olympics, made his debut at Madison Square Garden.

Joe Louis married cosmetics businesswoman Rose Morgan on Christmas Day in 1955. The following year, she sued him for an annulment on the grounds that he refused to have children with her. Her attorney tracked him down at a New York airport. The ex-champ was on his way to a golf tournament in Pittsburgh. He signed the annulment papers on the spot and boarded the plane.

In the late 1950s, Billy Rowe and Joe Louis formed the public relations firm Louis, Rowe, Lockhart, and Fisher at 250 West Fifty-seventh Street. One of their clients was the Cuban government. The firm signed a contract for $287,000 to attract blacks to the island of Cuba. According to Rowe, "The political chess game between the two governments has developed into a virtual war of words and political action here and in Cuba."

"Joe Louis was living in Las Vegas in the seventies," said a long-time Harlemite. "My old man was a gangster in those days. He and Joe Louis were good friends. My old man used to go out to Vegas and hang out with him. Joe needed money all the time. I used to wire thousands of dollars to Joe for my old man. Joe's money from him got cut off when he went to prison."

In a speech in the Skyline Ballroom at the Theresa Hotel in September 1950, Milton Webster, vice president of the Sleeping Car Porters union, said that African-Americans were consigned to menial positions, where the work is difficult and often dangerous and perilous to their health, the hours are overbearing, and the pay is cheap. Webster considered Joe Louis, Jackie Robinson, and Sugar Ray Robinson products of rare circumstances among African-Americans. "They brought us here in chains," Webster blasted, "and we're still in chains, and we must break them ourselves."

In 1954, Sugar Ray Robinson announced his decision to return to the ring. Gone were the glory days when Bill Brown used to hide Ray Robinson in a suite so he could relax a few days before one of his big fights. After a Robinson win, there would be the big light outside Sugar Ray's bar and grill that was so bright, it made Seventh Avenue look like daytime. When Sugar Ray Robinson made his announcement, *Amsterdam News* columnist Joe Bostic reminded readers that Ray had made $100,000 dancing the year before: "That, I thought, ought to keep a fellow safely off the relief roles. But, despite such a banner year, here he was saying he could use a buck." Although he claimed he could use a buck, he denied that he was broke. Robinson told the press that he was coming back to the ring to set an all-time precedent. He was going to be the first champion ever to retire and regain the title. Nobody believed Robinson's explanation. He was broke. "It was pretty clear that Sugar Ray was in trouble with his businesses," recalled Judge James Watson.

"Sugar Ray was riding high like a king when he first opened that bar and grill," said Marjorie Corbitt. "Edna Mae's aunt Blanche did all the cooking. The food was good. Everybody talked about how good Blanche Holly could cook. His place was around the corner from the hotel on Seventh Avenue. He owned the whole block. There was a barbershop that specialized in processing black men's hair—you know, the conk. Edna Mae had a lingerie shop in the block."

"I went to Sugar Ray's bar and grill—this was just before he closed down," said longtime Harlemite Yvonne Benjamin. "It was in the sixties and Liz Taylor and Richard Burton were in there. Liz had her shoes off while she was eating fried chicken. I took a picture of her. Lots of entertainers used to be in Sugar Ray's. Frank Sinatra, Sammy Davis Jr., and all the Rat Pack group used to stop in there. His bar and grill was one of the most popular spots during the 1950s and 1960s."

Sugar Ray Robinson lived as fast and hard as Joe Louis. "Everywhere he went, he would drive his car, and this made him automatically conspicuous," said Ray Robinson II. "If it was parked outside a building, they knew he was there. The man didn't care; he had girls all over town. He got to know the doormen all over the city, and they would watch his car while he was upstairs taking care of his business. He was a combination of a goodwill ambassador and a sex god. . . . Sometimes he would . . . leave me in the lobby of the

Theresa Hotel, when Charlie Rangel was desk clerk, while he went out and checked his 'traps,' his various female partners."

"Edna Mae and Ray Robinson—they both made a lot of money during their marriage," recalled Debbie McDade. "Even after her Cotton Club days, Edna Mae did print modeling for Lucky Gold cigarettes and other companies. She was a pretty woman. Then she hooked Ray Robinson. He was a big catch. He bought her one of the most expensive mink coats I'd ever seen in those days. Sugar Ray bought a pink convertible Cadillac. Say he had it especially made. Edna Mae and her aunt Blanche would drive by the hotel with the top down. It's hard to forget that pink Cadillac because one of the Ink Spots had one—almost the same color and all. Edna Mae and her aunt used to drive by the Theresa almost every day just to show off. She was trying to act like a rich white lady—you know, like a lady of leisure. Sometimes she and her aunt would stop in the Theresa and go up to the mezzanine to Etienne's dress shop. Edna Mae just had to show us something she bought. When Ray got rid of Edna Mae, she didn't have a dime. All that showing off in that Cadillac. She had to take a job as a receptionist. By that time, she was too old to go back to that showgirl stuff. I don't know why Edna Mae didn't take some of Ray's money and put it away for herself. I don't know why she let Ray Robinson blow all the money. It made no sense. Edna Mae had to stay with friends for a while when she and Ray split up."

"I have a friend who knew Edna Mae well since the 1930s," said Marjorie Corbitt. "This friend lived in the Theresa. Edna used to visit her in the hotel. She told me that Edna Mae stopped by her hotel room while her young niece was visiting from out of town. She had to run an errand, so she left Edna Mae and her niece in the room. When she returned, Edna Mae had been chasing the girl around the room."

"That's why Sugar Ray was always beating Edna Mae's ass," said one longtime Harlemite. "He was always catching her with women."

"I'll tell you what is sad," said Debbie McDade. "When I come to New York these days and see the old actresses and dancers out there still trying to make a dollar—trying to get dancing gigs—it pains me. Some of them didn't think that their looks would fade and the money would dry up. When I was young, it was hard to believe that the years would go by so fast. We don't feel that it will happen to us. We think we have all the time in the world. We don't feel those vulnerabilities. That's what happened to too many entertainers. Many of them don't have health insurance today. Now many of them are old and sick. Some of them have so much pride too. When I asked them to come to visit me, they can't afford it. They don't have a pension plan. Their social security checks are the minimum. The same with the male musicians. It's like they never thought they would get old. Many of them are still trying to dance and sing, and it's too late for all that. The Theresa days are gone. But some still want to live in that era."

"I knew the actress Francine Everett was a beautiful woman," said a long time Harlemite. "When her looks faded, she went to Harlem Hospital and worked as an aide. She got herself a pension plan before it was too late. A few others went to work before it got too late. The old showgirl Belle Powell—Adam Powell's first wife. He walked away from her for Hazel Scott and never looked back. Belle became a teacher's assistant. She did all right for herself."

"I recently saw another old resident of the Theresa, a show-girl from out of Durham, North Carolina," said a Harlem businesswoman. "I went to her apartment not long ago. She's in her seventies—maybe seventy-five. Lord, that woman's got a body like a thirty-year-old. She's posing nude. I mean she's having photographs taken of herself in the nude. She's getting paid for them. I don't know how she keeps herself looking so good, but she does. I didn't believe her until she showed me the photographs. These women still got hustle in 'em. She tried to convince me how I could make some money. I got out of there fast."

Rumors about Ray and Edna Mae Robinson weren't the only whispers of hard times spreading around the hotel. The gossip among local boxers and fans in the Theresa bar was about the stories Billy Rowe wrote about the Boston fighter known as Tar Baby (Sam Langford), who was now old, blind, and broke. He was forced to live on $1.65 per day. A number of old-timers remembered stories they heard about Langford's fight and loss by a decision to Jack Johnson in the old Douglas Athletic Club in downtown Chelsea. The Langford fund was set up to help the down-and-out boxer.

In a 1952 column, Billy Rowe told his readers of a rumor he had heard from sidewalk captain Maceo Birch: the Theresa Hotel had fallen on hard times. But Rowe and Birch found that rumor hard to accept because of the housing shortage in Harlem. This shortage caused a number of new people to make the hotel their year-round residence. Rowe pointed out that the slick boys were still driving their Cadillacs along the avenue.

Maceo Birch was more puzzled by the shysters who had disappeared from the corner outside the hotel, especially at sundown.

The suspense was cleared up when the Shalimar Club's owner, Red Randolph, told Birch that the new police commissioner had chased the numbers takers into hiding and threatened to lock up all hoodlums on the corner. A federal law was enforced requiring a $50 tax and 10 percent of gross monthly receipts from Harlem's numbers racket. This federal law scared the takers out of their skin and drops shut down, especially at Seventh Avenue and 125th Street, one of three main drops in Harlem. "The town is flooded with new social security cards that are being flashed at the glint of a badge by characters who heretofore took work very lightly, and would much rather let Mamye do the breadwinning; make it on the turn of a pair of dice, a deck of cards or the mag that just couldn't lose." After a few days passed, things outside on the Theresa's corner returned to normal. The new police commissioner eased the pressure, and things cooled down. The bankers, writers, and runners were back in business, and everyone was breathing a sigh of relief.

The sidewalk captains were huddling together trying to figure out who'd step in for the recently incarcerated Bumpy Johnson. The question was also on the lips of both races in the underworld. In 1953, Bumpy was arrested and tried and given the maximum sentence of fifteen years and a $9,000 fine for narcotics sales and conspiracy charges. Everybody in Harlem knew that his partner Nat Pettigrew was already serving fifteen to twenty. Who was going to step into the patent leather shoes of the irreplaceable Johnson as Harlem's king of the underworld? There was the legendary gangster Big Joe Richards. Rumors circulated of a gang war for supremacy. But Joe Richards faded from sight. The word on the street was that he made a deal with the FBI. Big Joe was now playing on the legitimate team to save his hide. Who had the courage to stand up to the powerful white East side mafia to claim the lion's share of sales from narcotics and numbers banking?

"Bumpy Johnson had always stood up to white mobsters like Dutch Schultz and Lucky Luciano," said Danny Moore. "That's why he was so powerful in Harlem. He was aided by the Gallo brothers. They were Italian gangsters. That's why Schultz didn't bother Bumpy, 'cause he had the powerful Gallo brothers behind him. Chink Cunningham and Johnny Walker were in the pocket of Schultz. They were like mafia field Negroes to Schultz 'cause Schultz was calling the shots. He was keeping the cops off his Negro bankers. He was making sure he got the percentage that he demanded. But Bumpy wasn't going to play the role of field Negro for no white mafia."

Bumpy was fearless. Helen Lawrenson was with Bumpy one night in a Harlem restaurant. A gangster took a shot at him while he was eating dinner. He got up from the table, went outside, and fired back at his would-be assassin. According to Lawrenson, Bumpy returned to the table and calmly finished his meal. He then ordered a banana split for dessert.

"Bumpy's friends tried to sell me his custom-made, black Lincoln Continental when he went to prison," said Danny Moore. "But, hell, I was too scared to buy it. I think the narcotics dealer Red Dillion bought it. Dillion certainly couldn't fill Bumpy's shoes. He wasn't fearless like Bumpy."

While Harlem's underworld was thinking about Bumpy's turf, the sidewalk captains told Billy Rowe that Hazel Scott, Lena Horne, and Langston Hughes were listed as Communist sympathizers. Scott's alleged Communist ties caused several interested sponsors of her potential television show to back away. Billy Rowe argued that these tactics by the government were about the most un-American thing that has ever been concocted. The producers of the smear campaign were damaging the reputations of people who really believed that there was no red other than the red in red, white, and blue. Lena Horne Hayten and Langston Hughes gathered their resources to defend themselves against the charges, which listed them among its collection of Communists and fellow travelers. Lena Horne Hayten was so angry that she almost blew a fuse while in Paris when she got the news that as an American, she had to defend her loyalty to her country.

"Things were hot in the hotel in the 1950s," recalled Danny Moore. "Ruth Brown was going with Jackie Wilson and me at the same time, and she was married to the great saxophone player Earl Swanson. Ruth was a Virginia girl. She was the first female rhythm-and-blues singer. She was one of the biggest celebrities in the 1950s. I met her in Cincinnati, but we were living in the Theresa at the time and didn't see each other that much. Her hit songs were '5-10-15 Hours' and '(Mama) He Treats Your Daughter Mean.' She had hit after hit. She made Atlantic Records. You know how they say Capitol Records is the house that Nat King Cole built? Well, Atlantic Records is the house that Ruth Brown built. Jackie Wilson knew about me and Ruth Brown. But Ruth decided she wanted me. So we began living together in the Theresa. Jackie Wilson was real nice about it. He was a nice cat. Later on, she divorced Swanson. We were together for a long time. She lives in Las Vegas now."

Billy Guy, a member of the popular 1950s singing group the Coasters, found himself in the midst of a scandal and the centerpiece of hotel gossip. He was pulled from his bed in the hotel one morning by New York City policemen. He was arrested on the spot. Handcuffed, he was charged with having sex with a sixteen-year-old white girl. Her mother signed the complaint, although the alleged victim said the sexual relation was consensual. Word spread like wildfire. The twenty-three-year-old singer was escorted down the elevator into the lobby, where crowds had formed and spilled onto Seventh Avenue. Guy was thrown into the backseat of a police car and hauled off to jail. At the same time, the Coasters were riding high on their hit songs "Yakity Yak" and "Charlie Brown."

"You know, Billy Guy is dead," said Danny Moore. "I see one of the Coasters regularly. It breaks my heart. The cat's got emphysema, and he's begging for a cigarette. I guess it doesn't matter at this point. I give him cigarettes when I see him.

" 'Do the Hucklebuck, do the Hucklebuck,' " sang Danny. "Remember that song? That was Paul Williams. He lived in the Theresa in the fifties too. I remember this: Paul got into some trouble. I think he came from Detroit. Anyway, he got into an automobile accident. His Caddy was torn up. One of his band members was killed. Williams was responsible for the accident. He was in some legal jam. He was being sued—seem like some kind of civil case. If he had gone back to Detroit, he would have been arrested. So he never went back. I think Paul just died a few years ago in a nursing home someplace over in Jersey."

"There was the trumpet player, can't think of his name. He was driving a car around Harlem," said Marjorie Corbitt. "There was an accident and that gorgeous showgirl Daisy Mae Richards got hurt. She was paralyzed after the accident. She was dating the driver of the car. After the accident, he dropped her like a hot potato. Moms Mabley helped to support Daisy Mae Richards. After Daisy Mae was released from the hospital, Moms put her up in the Theresa.

"Moms and I met two or three times a week and played pinochle in Daisy Mae's room," recalled musician Al Cobbs. "We'd play, Daisy Mae in bed and Moms and me sitting up on the side. Moms cheated all the time."

Mabley kept a room in the hotel the year round. During the time Moms Mabley was caring for Daisy Mae, she filmed a picture called *Killer Diller* with Butterfly McQueen. In the late 1950s, Daisy Mae returned to her native Texas. The judge awarded her a settlement from the musician who caused the car accident. She was never paid.

"The two brothers Red [Wilbert] and Arthur Prysock lived in the hotel," recalled Danny Moore. "They were tall and handsome. Even the women whistled at them when they walked down the street. Used to drive them gals crazy. They were some well-dressed brothers. Red Prysock had a red Cadillac convertible. Used to see him cruising up and down Seventh Avenue. That boy loved red. Red Prysock was a sax player. Red and Arthur did gigs together and recordings. I saw Arthur Prysock some years ago. It was in the early 1990s, I think. He was raggedy—talking all crazy. I thought he was drunk. Arthur was always well put together—you know, the way he dressed. But I couldn't figure out why he looked so bad. Later, I heard that he had Alzheimer's disease. He died a few years after that."

"Pee Wee Marquette left the Braddock and moved into the Theresa sometime in the mid 1950s" said Marjorie Corbitt. "That's when he was emceeing at Birdland downtown. The Birdland was one of the hottest nightspots in New York. Between his usual spot in front of the hotel and his job at the Birdland, he was keeping Izzy Rowe busy with news from the Birdland. Pee Wee was bigger than ever. He had been emceeing in Harlem, now he was downtown. He was in the big time. That little midget's ego got out of control. Pee Wee was strange. His size was so shocking. You'd hear this voice that sounded so good on the radio, never even thinking that he was a midget. He introduced the biggest artists of the day—Nat King Cole, Charlie Parker, Mary Lou Williams, Sarah Vaughan, and Billie Holiday. He traded on his position by letting people who could do something for him in the club."

The Birdland was replete with stories on the celebrities. The disc jockey Hal Jackson told the story of running into Tina Turner backstage just minutes before she was due onstage. Her face was bleeding from a number of blows from Ike Turner. By the time their act came up, she had covered her bruises with makeup. "There was a preponderance of drug use at the Birdland among black entertainers," recalled Hal Jackson. When Charlie Parker and Dizzy Gillespie were at Birdland for a week, Pee Wee Marquette said that Dizzy was the biggest draw—the main attraction. Billy Rowe gave Harry Belafonte and Lennie Tristano rave reviews for a show at the popular Birdland, the new home of happy music. Billy Rowe reported that the cool Erroll Garner, in great café society style, opened at Birdland and kept the audience in a trance. For a packed house, Illinois Jacquet let the hot dripping melody flow from his tenor sax.

On a spring day in 1951, the Theresa was host to Josephine Baker. Harlem had declared May 20 Josephine Baker Day. An estimated one hundred thousand people turned out on Seventh Avenue to welcome her. The parade was planned by the NAACP. The procession made its way to the Golden Gate Ballroom, where Ralph Bunche was on hand to present Baker an award for her work against prejudice in the theater. The festivities were continued at the Savoy Ballroom, where she was greeted by her hosts Charlie and Bessie Buchanan. Baker was entertained by Duke Ellington and the singer Thelma Carpenter, funnyman Timmie Rogers, and actress Juanita Hall. Among the guests at the Savoy were the Walter Whites, Fredi Washington, Adam Clayton Powell Jr., and Hazel Scott. The festivities throughout the day and night made the forty-five-year-old diva weary. She returned to the Hotel Theresa that night, where throngs of her fans lined both sides of Seventh Avenue to glimpse the exhausted French diva.

The following year, the radio stations WLIB and WWRL moved their complete broadcast operation to the second floor of the Theresa Hotel. In its new location, the broadcast operation was called Harlem's Hotel Theresa Radio Center. The major portion of the programming was aimed at black audiences. Disc jockey Hal Jackson had joined the staff of WLIB in 1949. He left before the year ended. Jackson returned to the station in 1953 when the station was airing from the Hotel Theresa. He brought his program, *The House That Jack Built*, which he had started for another station.

"I took advantage of the magic of radio to create an imaginary house as the setting for my show," said Hal Jackson. "*The House That Jack Built* was the era of 'personality radio,' and the most important thing a successful host did was to create a personality and the setting to go with it. In my imagination—and in that of my listeners—it was a large, comfortable home with a spacious living room and a terrace, an upstairs and downstairs. I'd open the show with 'How are you? This is Hal Jackson, the host that loves you most, welcoming you to *The House That Jack Built*. We're rolling out the musical carpet, and we'll be spinning a few just for you. So come on in and sit back, relax, and enjoy your favorite recording stars from here to Mars.' I chose all the records myself, although Richard Eaton made it clear that I was to stick to those by black artists— race music, as it was called then. I played Nat Cole and Dinah Washington and the Ink Spots because they were great artists. As I introduced each record, I pretended I was wandering around my imaginary house."

By this time, race music was also called rhythm and blues. A lot of disc jockeys on local Harlem stations were playing it. Hal Jackson pointed out that rhythm and blues and rock 'n' roll were resisted. A number of leading celebrities voiced their dislike for the genres, including Frank Sinatra and Nat King Cole. The new sound was as controversial as bebop had been nearly ten years earlier. The so-called race music was well received by WLIB listeners. "Berry Gordy and Marv Johnson came by the Theresa's WLIB studios just to say hello, and Berry and I took to each other immediately," said Hal Jackson. At the time, Berry was working for one of the automobile companies in Detroit as an assembly-line worker. He was writing songs for Jackie Wilson in his spare time. By the late 1950s, Gordy had founded Hitsville USA in Detroit. Hal Jackson credits Gordy for selecting artists and creating a rhythm-and-blues beat that appealed to audiences beyond black Americans.

"It was in the late 1950s that I got to know Malcolm X, the charismatic minister of Muslim Temple No. 7 in Harlem," said Hal

Ruth Ellington James with unidentified couple on the Hotel Theresa's mezzanine floor, 1950s. *Courtesy of Ophelia DeVore.*

Jackson. "I interviewed him quite a few times while broadcasting from the Hotel Theresa on WLIB and on WWRL. Malcolm was always candid when discussing his agenda for African-Americans, his struggle to gain respect for blacks in this country. He wanted blacks to accept and act on a renewed sense of self-worth and dignity. He hated the second-class-citizen mentality, and he wouldn't even talk to you if he felt you were still groveling and talking old junk."

WLIB news director Clifford Evans developed an interesting agenda that centered on community-affairs programs. As part of a community-affairs program, NAACP executive secretary Walter White came to the Theresa Hotel once a week to host a nationally syndicated talk show. Walter White kept his listeners informed on a variety of subjects, particularly the civil rights agenda of the NAACP. During his weekly shows, he interviewed a number of distinguished guests, including Ralph Bunche, Thurgood Marshall, Herbert Lehman, Josephine Baker, Adam Clayton Powell Jr., Mary McLeod Bethune, Jesse Owens, and Whitney Young. Year-round hotel resident Anna Arnold Hedgeman was a regular guest on White's show. She was the first woman of color in Mayor Robert Wagner's cabinet.

In one show, Walter White told his WLIB listeners that the so-called final report of Mayor Impelliteri's Committee on Unity in the Josephine Baker Stork Club case was "inexplicably fantastic." The report found "nothing to substantiate a charge of racial discrimination." White retaliated on Baker's behalf by writing the governor informing him that Sherman Billingsley had violated the Volstead Act, which made him ineligible for liquor license.

In 1954, Walter White called on every church, school, newspaper, trade union, parent-teachers' association, educational group, and business group to work incessantly for acceptance of the Supreme Court's decision to avert violence over school desegregation. He explained that the year 1954 marked the most publicized and important work of the NAACP, which was the legal attack on segregated education. But the road ahead included continued attacks on discrimination in housing, employment, transportation, and parks and other public areas.

By this time, Billy Rowe had left the *Courier* and Dan Burley had left the *Amsterdam News*. Other reporters were on the Harlem—Hotel Theresa beat: Geri Majors, Earl Brown, James Booker, and Earl Bostic of the *New York Amsterdam News*; Major Robinson of the *Chicago Defender*; and Izzy Rowe of the *Pittsburgh Courier*.

In 1954, Billy Rowe handed his column to his wife, Izzy, his retirement gala was held at the elegant Paul Schlosser's Paradise Club. "The Notebook" was a dramatization produced by Ossie Davis and Mervyn Nelson. The twenty-minute production included a skit that presented Rowe in his offices and his meanderings around the Hotel Theresa. On hand to offer praises to Rowe were New York City mayor Vincent Impelliteri, Ethel Waters, Duke Ellington, Sarah Vaughan, Ed Sullivan, George Treadwell, and Adam Clayton Powell Jr. Rowe's press colleagues like Major Robinson, Evelyn Cunningham, and Allan MacMillan were there. He was given a citation for "his unselfish commitment to entertainers of every stripe, his untiring devotion to justice and informed reporting."

Izzy Rowe wrote under the headline "Izzy's Notebook." Theresa regulars and residents had the Theresa bar sizzling about the wealth of news in the *Courier* as Izzy Rowe took over "Billy Rowe's Notebook." They said the juice was all there on the sons and daughters of Harlem. For instance: Joe Louis was rumored to be ready to wed after his fight with Marciano. . . . Sugar Ray was to have a gig to dance in the Palladium in London and had sold the rights to his life story to 20th Century Fox. . . . And a quite sizable group of cuties who lived in the Theresa had already decided what they would be wearing as they caught "Yardbird" Parker and Dizzy Gillespie for their act the coming weekend downtown at Birdland and Ray Robinson's act at Smalls' Paradise.

In another column, without naming her intended, Izzy asked if it was true that a particular black bandleader had divided his gathering down the middle by seating his white and light members along with the road managers on one side of the bus while the darker ones sat on the other side.

According to her, bandleader Lucky Millinder was one of the busiest men in the hotel. He was the bandleader during *Amateur Hour* every Wednesday night at the Apollo Theater. He was seen running along West 125th Street between the Apollo and the Hotel Theresa every evening. He had no time for conversation.

"Lucky Millinder took an integrated band down to Charleston, South Carolina, during this time," recalled trumpet player Joe Wilder. "There were three white players in the band. The rest were colored. When they got to Charleston, the club owner told Lucky that he wasn't going to have an integrated band playing in his club. The engagement was canceled. Lucky said, 'This isn't an integrated band. We're all colored.' The club owner looked over at the three white musicians. 'You colored?' he asked each one. 'Yes, sir,' they each answered. They kept the engagement and didn't have no trouble down there."

In 1950 Richard Wright returned to New York after spending nearly a year in Buenos Aires, Argentina. There he had produced a movie based on his book *Native Son* and starred in the lead role of Bigger Thomas. Thin and fatigued after months of arduous film work, Wright said his movie was likely one of the most well-done films produced in Latin America in years.

By 1951, Ella Fitzgerald's relationship with her husband, Ray Brown, had terminated. In her column, Izzy explained that it's really tough when romance is off again, and Ella and her hubby had decided that it was just not to be. It was particularly rough on both of them because they were with "Jazz at the Philharmonic," and they had to spend time together even though they weren't speaking.

Pigmeat Markham took a big role in Mike Myerberg's musical Henry Nemo's *Hot Rocks*. This musical included Langston Hughes. "Pig's wife, Mary, used to pawn her engagement ring every time she and Pig had money problems," said Naidine Collins. "They lived in the Braddock Hotel for the longest. When Pig would get a royalty check or some work, they would go and get the ring out of hock."

Major Robinson joined the staff of *Jet* in 1957. He scooped a story on Theresa guests Prophet Jones and his entourage. A number of New York reporters waited all day at the ritzy Park Sheraton Hotel for Jones and his group to check into the hotel's $75 per day suites. But all the while they were waiting, Jones and company were relaxing in the Hotel Theresa in $7 per day suites.

The following year, gossips in the hotel were on pins and needles waiting to learn the fate of the marriage of Bill Brown and his estranged wife, Gloria. The two had been seen around Harlem on several dates. The word in the hotel grapevine was they were reconciling. But to the delight a number of females in the Hotel Theresa, there was no reconciliation.

The hotel rumor mill was buzzing with more scandalous stories.

Ophelia DeVore fashion show in the Hotel Theresa, 1950s. *Courtesy of Ophelia DeVore.*

The members of the Platters, a popular rhythm and blues singing group, were charged with aiding and abetting prostitution. They were found by police with three nude white women in a Cincinnati hotel. Although the women were gainfully employed and no cash was exchanged, the head of the Cincinnati police unit said they had just met. That was enough to charge the women with prostitution. The attorney for the Platters declared that it was an invasion of privacy. The case against the Platters was eventually thrown out of court.

Some good news in the midst of the Platters scandal was that hotel resident and opera singer Merritt Hedgeman had received great reviews for his performance in *The Evening of Spirituals*. In the audience was a high-powered record executive who signed him on the spot.

The Savoy Ballroom closed in 1958. It had been the pleasure dance hall to millions in its thirty-two-year history. It had brought joy to the lives of European royalty, Hollywood superstars, national politicians, and everyday people. Its old Steinway piano that had been played by Nat King Cole, Fats Waller, Duke Ellington, Chick Webb, and Count Basie sold at auction for $450.

"With the passing of the Savoy Ballroom, a part of show business is gone," said Count Basie. "I feel about the same way I did when someone told me the news that Bill 'Bojangles' Robinson was dead."

By the time the Savoy closed, Count Basie had opened a nightclub on Seventh Avenue and 132nd Street. There was live music. The popular spot catered to all ages. "You'd find gangsters, professionals, and regular working people in Basie's place," said longtime

Harlemite Jake McKnight. Basie had major acts there like Eddie 'Lockjaw' Davis. "There was always a white crowd," said musician Danny Moore. "But the upper class went to the Red Rooster. That was on Seventh Avenue and 137th Street. You'd find your politicians, doctors, and lawyers there. That was a place for Harlem's gentlemen. The first time I went there, I was with Dr. Tracey Parks. He was like my big brother."

Smalls' Paradise was still going strong throughout the 1950s with its live music. The famous tap dancers were still hitting the floor. Nipsey Russell was keeping the audiences in stitches with his jokes at the Baby Grand. Sugar Ray Robinson's bar and grill was known for its steady stream of movie stars.

"I didn't want to leave Harlem in those days," said Jake McKnight. "There was nothing for me downtown. The nightlife was in Harlem."

"Ladies didn't go into places like the Red Rooster and Sugar Ray Robinson's nightclubs," said Jewel Sims Okala. "If there was an affair in Harlem and ladies attended, it was the Skyline Ballroom. The Skyline Ballroom was the nicest place we had in Harlem in late 1940s and early 1950s. I went to a number of events there. Ralph Bunche was honored there by the NAACP after he received the Nobel Peace Prize in 1950. It was an elegant evening. Thurgood Marshall, Dr. Louis T. Wright, Roy Wilkins, Walter White, Arthur Spingarn, Governor Lehman—the place was packed with notables. Merritt Hedgeman sang during the evening. Merritt Hedgeman was Anna Arnold Hedgeman's husband. She was a brilliant woman—just brilliant. They were living in the Theresa at the time. She and Merritt were our good friends.

An evening in the Hotel Theresa's Skyline Ballroom, 1950s. *Courtesy of Ophelia DeVore.*

"Merritt was really like the wife," said one of their friends. "He took care of the domestic side of their life. Anna was the hardworking politician and activist. But it worked for them. They were very happy."

"There were a number of weddings in the Skyline Ballroom. My niece's wedding reception was there. I thought Mr. Brown managed the Skyline Ballroom very well," said Jewel Sims Okala.

In 1954, the sidewalks on both sides of Seventh Avenue were lined with fans who came out to see the all-star cast from the movie *Carmen Jones*. Otto Preminger and Dorothy Dandridge were being honored by the black press and radio representatives in a reception in the Skyline Ballroom. Dandridge starred in the title role as Carmen Jones. She was honored with a plaque as the favorite screen star in a poll conducted by the national black press. Others in the cast who attended were Harry Belafonte, Pearl Bailey, Diahann Carroll, and Nick Stewart. Five hundred guests were invited, but fifteen hundred people turned out in the Skyline Ballroom. Attentive readers noted that when 20th Century Fox advertised *Carmen Jones* in black newspapers, it listed the names of Belafonte, Dandridge, Bailey, and others in the film, while the ads for the movie in white dailies omitted the names of the stars.

There were a number of elite clubs during the 1940s and 1950s. Your academic and social credentials were not easily called into question if you had membership in certain clubs. Bill Brown hosted a number of cotillions, dinners, charity events, and other formal gatherings in the Skyline Ballroom for the Guardsmen, Girl Friends, the Smart Set, Links, Delta Sigma Theta and Alpha Kappa Alpha sororities; Alpha Phi Alpha and Omega Psi Phi fraternities; and Les Douze. Childrens's clubs were Tom Thumb, and Jack and Jill. A young Ronnie Brown had membership in Tom Thumb.

"The clubs were more than just a means for fun and fantasizing," said the writer Stephen Holmes. "They confirmed your status as one of the best people. You heard about the latest job openings and kept track of who was moving up and who was moving down. Some taught social graces and networking skills and reinforced shared values."

"The Guardsmen sprang out of a group of guys who were in college at just about the same time, traditional black colleges and university," said Lawrence Douglas Wilder, the former governor of Virginia. "They made it as clear as possible that it was not founded to try to be a social action organization. It was never intended to be anything other than entertainment."

The New York chapter of the Guardsmen was made up of doctors, lawyers, and businessmen. A majority had gone to traditionally black colleges like Howard, Hampton, Morehouse, Morgan State, and Fisk. A number of male parties were had throughout the years, and the Guardsmen were never far from one another professionally. As Stephen Holmes noted years after the Theresa closed, Ron Brown and Doug Wilder crossed paths again.

"The Guardsmen used to fish at Sheepshead Bay on some Saturdays," recalled Bill's nephew Nick Jones. "They'd all come back to the hotel where they'd have a big fish fry."

"I held my graduations for models in Hotel Theresa each year beginning in 1946," said businesswoman Ophelia DeVore. "The early graduations were in the dining room on the first floor of the hotel. When the Skyline Ballroom opened in 1949, the graduations were held there until the 1960s. The young ladies who participated in the DeVore fashion shows in the hotel looked different from the girls who went into the bar. The DeVore students were only seen in the dining room or the Skyline Ballroom. White people had an image of women in Harlem—that we weren't refined, that black women in Harlem were prostitutes and whores. That was not true to start with. But I wanted to do something about the image of my people—to teach women about the social graces, how to dress for every occasion. A lady has to carry herself in a style to gain respect. That's important—the image one projects matters. I've always believed that the African-Americans were talented and equal in every way to any other group. But image is critical for any line of work one wants to pursue."

While a number of black women were trying to enhance their appearance by using bleaching creams to lighten their skin, the DeVore School made its mission to impress upon its students that black skin in all hues was beautiful. Long before the 1960s "black is beautiful" crusade, Ophelia DeVore recognized the need to make black women and men appreciated around the world. But first, they themselves had to believe in their own unique beauty. By the 1950s, Ophelia DeVore's models were winning beauty contests in Paris and other world capitals. She remembered her former top model Cecelia Cooper whom she took to Paris in 1959. Cecelia was selected by officials at the Cannes Film Festival that year to represent the festival's image. She was chosen among women from around the world, according to Ophelia DeVore. Cecelia's winning this honor helped to change the stereotype because a black American was chosen as the most beautiful woman at the Cannes Festival that year. Based on that achievement, she was given the Seat of Honor. "When Cecelia and I left New York, there were no reporters in sight," recalled Ophelia DeVore. "When we returned from Paris, they were all around us."

Graduates of the DeVore School include Helen Williams, Diahann Carroll, Cecely Tyson, and Jane White.

Like Ophelia DeVore, Dorothy Lamour had image on her mind. The actress, who starred in the movies *Typhoon* and *The Road to Singapore,* started a chain of cosmetics and beauty salons in the 1950s. Lamour opened an uptown branch office on the mezzanine floor of the Hotel Theresa.

Throughout the 1950s, the black-tie evenings in the Skyline Ballroom were giving the newspaper society reporters plenty to write about. The regulars and residents of the Hotel Theresa were stationed in their usual spots on the sidewalks and beneath the marquee when social clubs like the New York Smart Set and their guests arrived for the annual Spring Dance in the Skyline Ballroom. These members of Harlem society arrived in limos and Cadillacs. Their evenings usually benefitted such groups as the United Nations International Children's Emergency Fund.

Ophelia DeVore, 1940s. *Courtesy of Ophelia DeVore.*

Ten

THE INTERNATIONAL
SPOTLIGHT ON THE
HOTEL THERESA

Africa is the motherland of black America, and never was the sentiment more felt than in Harlem. The African in America suffered under a system of chattel slavery and then Jim Crow while Africans on the continent suffered under European imperialism. Consequently, black leaders across America related personally and politically to the struggles of African nations for independence; there had long been an understanding among a number of black leaders in America that the independence of Africa was vitally significant to the freedom of black Americans. "The only thing we wanted for our country was the right to a decent existence, to dignity without hypocrisy, to independence without restrictions . . . the day will come when history will have its say," wrote Patrice Lumumba, the premier of the independent Republic of the Congo. Lumumba's words could easily have been written by a black person in America. Over the years, propaganda had been fed to both Africans and black Americans to create rifts between the groups. That the United Nations was located in New York City gave black Americans, especially activists in Harlem, the opportunity to overcome divide-and-conquer rhetoric and to connect with African leaders. The unification of Africans and black Americans without the barrier of white propaganda was a critical factor, many believed, in the well-being and future of each group. The time had come for black Americans to correct the prevailing misconceptions about Africa in order to disclose the truth—and vice versa.

By the 1950s, leaders like Lumumba, Kwame Nkrumah, Julius Nyerere in Tanganyika, Tom Mboya in Kenya, and Sékou Touré were working toward building and unifying modern nations free from the shackles of colonialism. When black Americans met these talented African thinkers, they realized, as Malcolm X would have put it, "You been hoodwinked—you been had." African diplomats boldly spoke on the floor of the United Nations and on the corner of Seventh Avenue and 125th Street about African independence, and they talked about the mob violence against blacks across the South. That African leaders used a platform in front of the Hotel Theresa to address African independence and the ills of American racism was a clear indication of the hotel's prominence as black America's headquarters and of Harlem's significance as the black headquarters of the world. The lively sounds of conga and bongo drums enhanced the drama. Aromas of incense and food from pushcart vendors circled high in the air. And the backdrop was the famous Hotel Theresa.

Beginning in the late 1950s and throughout the 1960s, speaker after speaker like Malcolm X, Pork Chop Davis-Foreman, James Lawson, Carlos Cook, and Charles Kenyatta stood outside the Hotel Theresa in the midst of black American demonstrators rejecting the shackles of African colonialism. Black activists in America understood that a free Africa was vital to their interest.

Dr. Kwame Nkrumah, the first president of an independent Ghana in 1957, was educated at Lincoln University in Pennsylvania. When Nkrumah came to speak in front of the Hotel Theresa, black Americans carried placards that read, "U.N.—Stop Faking!" "Congo for the Congolese," "Dr. Bunche & His Bunch, When They Pulled That Stunt in South Africa."

When African leaders like Nkrumah joined forces with New York black nationalists to put the ills of colonialism and American racism before the world, this international movement made the Hotel Theresa the epicenter of activism for black peoples around the world.

When Fidel Castro made his famous visit to the Theresa in 1960, he stated that he too understood the African independence movement. He vowed to defend the Congo's Patrice Lumumba and hoped to learn many lessons during his stay, particularly while at the United Nations. "They are exploited and suppressed just as we are," Castro said during his James Booker interview. "The new nations and we in Latin America are all African-Americans."

Fidel Castro was in New York City to address the United Nations for the first time. The Cuban delegation checked into the Shelburne Hotel downtown on Thirty-seventh Street and Lexington Avenue, after being refused admittance by a number of other hotels downtown. Complaining that the Cuban delegation was rowdy, the Shelburne management demanded an advance payment of $10,000. An infuriated Castro refused to put down an advance and decided to leave. Another story circulating around Harlem is that the managers at the Shelburne asked Castro to leave after learning he had brought live chickens to the hotel. They feared he intended to use the chickens for voodoo rituals.

• • •

James Booker was privileged to participate in Castro's historic visit to the Hotel Theresa. He recalled talking to the African nationalist James Lawson one day in 1960. "Lawson told me that Fidel Castro was coming to Harlem to stay at the Theresa that same evening. I was a bit surprised, but I knew Lawson had seen Castro downtown earlier that day. It was September nineteenth, 1960.

"Lawson's lineage was part Cuban. He had traveled to the island country on several occasions and had met with Castro when he was there. So I figured that he was telling the truth. Castro was in New York for the World Meeting of the United Nations. He expressed to Lawson that he was not receiving satisfactory accommodations while at the Shelburne Hotel downtown. Lawson suggested that he come to *the Theresa*."

According to manager Love B. Woods, a group of officials from the Fair Play for Cuba Committee had called to see if he would and could accept Castro and his entourage of eighty. Woods had quickly said yes and offered them inducements to come to the Theresa.

Woods had been managing hotels since 1921. He had been at the Hotel Theresa since the spring before Castro's arrival. For him, the Castro delegation's impromptu appearance didn't cause the slightest unease.

Castro directed his motorcade uptown to the Hotel Theresa. Welcomed by Love B. Woods, the Cubans were delighted to be well received in Harlem. Castro and his entourage of eighty were installed on the ninth and tenth floors of the Theresa. They were given eighty rooms at a total price of $800 per day.

Fidel Castro. *Courtesy of Evelyn Cunningham.*

White journalists from *Time, Newsweek,* and other major publications were clamoring for interviews, but Castro said he would not speak to any white reporters until after his United Nations speech. He granted interviews to two black reporters prior to his United Nation's speech: James Booker and Carl Nesfield. Their interviews with Castro were published in the *Amsterdam News* and the *New York Age.* Shortly after Castro checked into the Theresa, Booker, Nesfield, and Malcolm X and his delegation had been ushered into Castro's suite. Castro proclaimed, "I had always wanted to come to Harlem, but I was not sure what kind of welcome I would get. When I got news that I would be welcomed in Harlem, I was happy . . . I feel very warm here."

"The first thing Castro said to Malcolm was 'Where's your bodyguard?' " said Preston Wilcox.

"Now that you're in Harlem, do you feel any better than if you were still at a downtown hotel?" James Booker asked Castro.

"I feel like I were in Cuba," Castro said.

He gave James Booker a forty-minute interview in his ninth-floor suite about one hour after arriving in the Theresa.

"They will think Castro is doing it for propaganda, but when they gave me the opportunity to come, I did," Castro said, commenting on his presence in the Theresa. "It is marvelous that even though you get propaganda all day in the newspapers and on radio and television, you still understand. This is wonderful, very interesting.' In Castro's suite, he and Malcolm X greeted each other like two heads of state.

"Castro has always been working against all kinds of discrimination in Cuba, and we will not stand for any kind of discrimination,"

Castro said. "All people are alike to us in Cuba. We have been trying to get more Negroes to come to Cuba."

The Cuban leader made it plain that he would not be speaking in Harlem, but he would speak out at the United Nations against discrimination. He feared if he spoke in Harlem, he would be accused of getting involved in affairs that were unrelated to him or his government.

Castro passed out Cuban cigars to everyone in the room and gave each of them a signed speech that he had given.

He rejected Malcolm X's offer to have dinner at the Muslim restaurant on 116th Street. The Cuban leader said he would prefer to take all of his meals in the Theresa. He noted, "Our people are changing. We are one of the most free in the world. We hope all peoples can meet and solve the problems soon of discrimination."

As Castro indicated to those in the room, including Malcolm X, that he was tired, his visitors stood to bid the weary Cuban leader good-night. Malcolm X and Castro shook hands. Castro invited him to Cuba at his expense.

The news of Castro being in Harlem spread like wildfire. "In moments, we were on the street in the rain, finding cabs or private cars or heading for subways. We were going to welcome the Cubans to Harlem," recalled Maya Angelou. "To our amazement, at eleven o'clock on a Monday evening, we were unable to get close to the hotel. Thousands of people filled the sidewalks and intersections, and police had cordoned off the main and side streets. I hovered with my friends on the edges of the crowd, enjoying the Spanish songs, the screams of 'Viva Castro,' and the sounds of conga drums being played nearby in the damp night air."

"There were so many people on the street in front of the hotel and I remember it was raining," recalled the writer Rosa Guy. "Everybody was so happy and excited as they sang 'Castro, si' and 'Yankee, no.' There were blacks and Puerto Ricans, but mostly blacks.

"My friend and I were flirting. My friend was Marcey Lee McBroom. We managed to get inside. We wanted to get on Castro's floor and we did. But we got stopped by some of the hotel workers. There were other women around trying to get up to the rooms too. We tried to get to Castro's room. We tried to flirt with his soldiers to get inside, but it didn't work. We really wanted to get up to their rooms and meet some of those good-looking Cuban men. The Theresa was known for its wealthy clientele. Only wealthy black people could get in that day."

"Castro was especially nice to the laborers in the hotel. One evening he had the custodial staff as his guests for dinner," Evelyn Cunningham remembered. "I took a room in the hotel for four days just to write my story about him. The *Pittsburgh Courier*'s management sent word to me that they didn't have the money to pay for my hotel expenses, so I paid out of my own pocket because I knew this was a once-in-a-lifetime story and I needed to be in the hotel. I didn't interview him but I was there to observe him moving around the hotel and the neighborhood. The story about Castro bringing live chickens to the hotel is true. I saw the chickens. He had his people cook them in the hotel. He threw chicken feathers out the windows while waving to the huge crowds in the streets surrounding the hotel. Don't ask me why he threw the feathers out the window."

The hotel laborers had a different take on the attitude of Castro's entourage. Charles Beard, one of the hotel's bellmen, believed the Cubans were insensitive and cheap. "The Castro men ordered coffee and ice water fifteen to twenty times Monday night and haven't yet given me a dime," he said. "We need to convert this guy."

A few Harlemites who recall the famous Castro visit said Castro brought a planeload of prostitutes to the hotel. At the same time, a number of activists accused the media of spreading the rumor about prostitutes to undercut the credibility of Castro. The media accused Castro of paying people to come out in support of his visit. According to Robert DesVerney, "The reputation of the papers was so bad among the people in Harlem that the crowds would often scream 'yellow press' and throw pennies at the reporters."

"Oh, boy . . . everyone wanted to see Castro, it was the first time a leader of his political stature had done such a thing," said the writer Pedro Pérez Sarduy. "He didn't have to go to Harlem, if they didn't want him in the hotel where he was staying, he could have gone to another, but nobody ever thought he'd come to Harlem. . . . People came from all over to see Castro. . . . Streets were blocked, there was partying in all of Harlem because Castro came to speak to us and share with us his problems, which were similar. . . . For months people were talking about his visit. . . . I remember it like yesterday."

During Castro's week in Harlem, the streets were a virtual mob scene filled with reporters, policemen, Secret Servicemen. Castro occasionally strolled around the neighborhood, and these outings caused even more pandemonium.

The activist Robert DesVerney went to the Theresa every night during Castro's stay and wrote down copious notes on what he saw. He even copied the wording from the placards: "Fidel is welcome in

Harlem anytime"; "Cuba practices real democracy, not race discrimination"; "We need more Castros, fewer Uncle Toms." DesVerney's own sign that he held up outside the hotel read, "U.S. Jim Crows Fidel, just like U.S. Jim Crows U.S. Negroes!"

The Cuban journalist Reynaldo Penalver came to the Theresa to cover Castro's visit. He met Malcolm X, who thought he was West Indian. Penalver said that Malcolm X thought Cuba was an island of white people. After learning from Penalver that Cuba was extensively mixed, Malcolm suggested setting up a Muslim branch in Cuba.

During the next two nights, Castro entertained a series of visitors from the United Nations in the Theresa. One of the many stories circulating was that Castro was occupying so much of the news that he had upstaged the Soviet Union's leader, Nikita Khrushchev. The Soviet leader got back in the headlines by paying a visit to the Hotel Theresa himself two days after Castro's arrival. The police personnel in Harlem had been given only four minutes' notice of Premier Khrushchev's arrival. Khrushchev's surprise visit to Harlem created near pandemonium. The crowds were almost unmanageable. Those on the scene could not believe the historic event taking place before their eyes.

A *New York Times* reporter described it as the biggest event to hit the famous intersection since the funeral of W. C. Handy in 1958.

Maya Angelou described the sentiments of a number of black people on the streets when Khrushchev arrived on the scene: "Wasn't no Communist country that put my grandpappa in slavery. Wasn't no Communist lynched my poppa or raped my mamma.

"Hey, Khrushchev. Go on with your bad self."

"The symbols were absolutely magnificent," said the historian John Henrik Clarke. "Fidel Castro in a black-owned hotel, Khrushchev meeting him in the lobby, the community surrounding the hotel day and night. Castro occasionally coming to the window to wave. It was an event in the development of consciousness in the community."

Maya Angelou said when Khrushchev came to the Theresa, the white policemen were nervous as they guarded the intersection of Seventh Avenue and 125th Street. The visit of Khrushchev to the Theresa was filled with excitement and drama. "It's been the biggest thrill of my lifetime, and I guess the only thing I can say is that I am pleased," said Love B. Woods.

Khrushchev, speaking for the Soviet Union, denounced Dag Hammarskjold, secretary general of the United Nations, saying that Hammarskjold was in favor of the imperialist powers in Africa and that he refused to confer with the central government of the Congo.

Outside the hotel, numerous factions were in the crowd. Some chanted "Yellow press, yellow pres, cha cha cha." There were thousands of Muslims, whose signs spoke for them: "Allah is the greatest." A number in the crowd were delighted to have Castro in New York expressing his anti-American rhetoric. Adam Clayton Powell Jr. believed that Castro was using blacks in Harlem to help stage a black revolution in America that he planned to direct from Cuba.

By the time Castro arrived at the Theresa in 1960, the neighborhood was a bastion of black nationalism. There was Lewis Micheaux's bookstore. Micheaux was a black nationalist, and the vast majority of books he sold were of that persuasion. The well-known black nationalist organization the Harlem Labor Center was a couple of blocks from the hotel. The Nation of Islam had several newspaper publishing outfits in the neighborhood.

In the midst of the excitement, a Cuban flag was temporarily raised on top of the Hotel Theresa's marquee. The Cubans in New York proclaimed that the employees of the fashionable Hotel Riviera in Havana would change its name to the Hotel Theresa in honor of Castro's visit. The name change never happened. It was all part of Castro's hype.

Evelyn Cunningham viewed Castro as a hypocrite. She recalled, "He came to Harlem professing his gratitude and affection for our people. But I had traveled to Cuba on a number of occasions and interviewed people close to Castro. I saw no dark-skinned Cubans with visible service jobs like chambermaids, waitresses, or clerks. Those jobs were all given to white Cubans. I thought that was very telling. Castro had to know this. How could he not know something that was so visible? All the while he was in the Theresa, he couldn't stop talking about his love for Harlem and its people and all that. I couldn't accept that knowing what I saw in Cuba."

It has been said that Castro called his predecessor Fulgencio Batista a *negro de mierda,* a "shitty nigger." In Castro's army, 90 percent of the soldiers were black. Yet, 95 percent of his high-ranking officers were white Cubans. It has made people wonder if James Booker's headline in the *Amsterdam News,* "Is Castro a Convertible?" during Castro's Harlem visit was befitting.

Carlos Moore acted as an interpreter between Castro and the Theresa manager. In a letter to Carlos Moore, Pedro Pérez Sarduy wrote, "The Cuban leader's visit to that hotel had caused a stir in political and diplomatic circles. That unexpected gesture of solidarity with the black civil rights community—what you call the Harlem Show—was never seen before in that upper Manhattan neighborhood."

When Castro returned to the United States in October 1995, he spoke at the Abyssinian Baptist Church, where over two thousand people were on hand to hear him. He recalled his visit to Harlem thirty-five years before: "I wanted to visit the Theresa Hotel, and I wanted to have an encounter with you here in Harlem. Those were uncomfortable days, when I came to the Theresa Hotel many years ago. There was such hostility, such a campaign against our country, that I passed through one district where people gestured like this [thumbs down]. I don't know what they meant by that, but I could imagine that something was wrong. But everything changed when I came to Harlem.

"Rosemari [Mealy] mentioned all the people who came to visit me at the Theresa Hotel in 1960, international leaders who were in solidarity with me. Khrushchev was one of the first leaders who came to visit me, and he was the leader of a superpower. I appreciated that gesture. Khrushchev was a very shrewd peasant, a very funny guy, and he didn't dismantle his country."

Back in 1960, the Cubans paid their Theresa bill and checked out. "Harlem citizens," the *Amsterdan News* reported, "breathed a sigh of relief." The *New York Times* asked the manager if he would like a another visit from the Cuban leader. "Compulsory, I would," answered Woods. "Voluntarily no."

Maya Angelou had recognized in the Theresa crowd her fourteen-year-old son, Guy, who had missed school that day without her permission. After she questioned him about his absence from school, the youngster replied, "Mother, I guess you'll never understand. To me, a black man, the meeting of Cuba and the Soviet Union in Harlem is the most important thing that could happen. It means that, in my time, I am seeing powerful forces get together to oppose capitalism. I don't know how it was in your time, the olden days, but in modern America this was something I had to see. It will influence my future."

Before Love B. Woods could recover from Castro and Khrushchev, a number of important dignitaries would be stopping by the Theresa as the 1960 presidential campaign was under way. Senator Henry Cabot Lodge, the Republican vice presidential candidate, and Mrs. Lodge stopped by the Hotel Theresa for a campaign rally. The Lodges were accompanied by Jackie Robinson and Judge Samuel R. Pierce and Rodman Rockefeller. A day later, the Democrats arrived at Seventh Avenue and 125th Street. Mrs. Robert Kennedy represented her brother-in-law, Democratic presidential candidate John F. Kennedy. She was accompanied by Mrs. Robert Wagner, the wife of New York city's mayor.

On October 12, 1960, John F. Kennedy, the Democratic candidate for president, arrived at the Hotel Theresa for a public rally. He was accompanied by his wife, Jacqueline, Eleanor Roosevelt, Adam Clayton Powell Jr., Senator Herbert Lehman, Governor Averell Harriman, and Mayor Robert Wagner.

"I am delighted to come and visit," Kennedy told the crowd. "Behind the fact of Castro coming to this hotel, Khrushchev coming to Castro, there is another great traveler in the world, and that is

Jacqueline Kennedy *(third from left)*, Congressman Adam Clayton Powell Jr. *(fourth from left)*, and Eleanor Roosevelt *(fifth from left)* attend a John F. Kennedy *(at podium)* presidential campaign rally in front of the Hotel Theresa, 1960.

the travel of a world revolution, a world in turmoil. I am delighted to come to Harlem and I think the whole world should come here and the whole world should recognize that we all live right next to each other, whether here in Harlem or on the other side of the globe."

Eleven

THE FINAL DAYS

In 1963, word reached the Theresa that one of its former residents, Dinah Washington, was dead. Rumors began to spread that the jazz diva had died from an overdose of pills. Some believed she had committed suicide, but her death was ruled accidental. "Dinah was always drinking and taking diet pills," said Danny Moore. "She was always trying to lose weight. Whatever new diet pill that came on the market, she took it. She kept the partying going."

The thirty-nine-year-old singer had been married six times. She was estranged from her husband at the time she died. Dinah put her husband out for cheating on her shortly before she died. She usually would have jumped on a man for something like that. But this guy was a black belt. She couldn't handle him. He went straight to the Hotel Theresa and got a room.

"Miss Epps told us in the coffee shop that Dinah Washington was dead," said Debbie McDade. "A sadness covered the hotel. That's all everybody talked about for days."

Jackie Wilson was shot that same year. One of Jackie's paramours shot him in the kidney. He survived, but the doctors were unable to remove the bullet. So he lived with it for the rest of his life. Jackie stayed in the Theresa when he was performing in New York.

Gossip in the Theresa was that Jackie had been shot because one woman had caught him with another. "Jackie was married, but they were estranged," said Danny Moore. "Jackie wasn't what I call a womanizer. A womanizer is a man who goes out and looks for a woman, hits on her. It wasn't like that with Jackie and a lot of those musicians. Women would be waiting backstage for Jackie. Tear his clothes off. He didn't have to go looking for a woman. See, I don't see that as a womanizer. There were women who would let themselves be passed around. There were all kinds of group sex."

At the end of 1960, Love B. Woods announced that the Hotel Theresa was undergoing major renovations to the tune of $100,000. Mr. Woods, the owner of the hotel and the manager, said that because of the international press that the hotel had generated because of Castro's visit, he had received correspondence from the dignitaries in the major world capitals congratulating him on his hotel's amenities. Woods further stated that he was delighted to know that such dignitaries were requesting reservations. It was his desire to make the Theresa as fine as any hotel downtown. His improvements included returning telephones to each of the three hundred rooms, additional private baths, and added services for the dining room. He planned to reopen the hotel's famous bar and add the gold lounge.

Songwriter and singer Billy Vera started out at the Apollo and knew many of the musicians who did business in the hotel. "There was a gold lounge in the Theresa in the sixties," recalled Vera. "There was an office nearby with a telephone which was connected to the police precinct. If there was a buzz, they knew that the police were warning them that there was going to be a cocaine bust. Redd Foxx's sidekicks used to score cocaine for him in the gold lounge. In the 1960s, coke was considered a rich man's drug. During the day, normal folks would be in the bar drinking, but after seven, pimps and sporting types entered the hotel. It had become the place that respectable entertainers no longer wanted to stay. The Motown singers were staying downtown at the President's Hotel. But the Theresa was a good place to cop drugs. The gold lounge was one of the places that rich white men and upper echelons made their connections."

Love B. Woods had spent his entire fortune trying to maintain the hotel. "He was an old man maybe in his eighties trying to run the Theresa," recalled Marjorie Corbitt. "He was practically senile. Every hotel he owned turned into a cathouse. He was doing the same thing to the Theresa."

The nightclubs in Harlem began to close in the late 1950s and the 1960s. The Theresa was central to the nightlife in Harlem. Mainly pimps and prostitutes were frequenting the Theresa's bar. The Red Rooster was now the gathering place for the old Theresa bar crowd and the younger professionals. Smalls' Paradise was now owned by the basketball player Wilt Chamberlain. The King Curtis band was a regular feature there. A number of Chamberlain's friends from the sports world frequented the club. Nevertheless, it didn't enjoy the popularity that it once had. The Apollo was still going strong. Singers like Jackie Wilson, Martha and the Vandellas, Little Anthony and the Imperials, and the Crystals were drawing a new generation to the famous theater.

In 1964, the entertainment community in New York and Los Angeles were saddened by the sudden death of Willie Bryant. He was found dead in his Los Angeles home by his friend and producer

Leonard Reed. The fifty-six-year-old stage and radio personality was the victim of a heart attack. Willie Bryant was considered a son of Harlem. Bryant, who was a popular radio talk show host and disc jockey in Harlem for more than thirty-years, was the "unofficial mayor of Harlem."

Percy Sutton (*left*) and Malcolm X (*surrounded by bodyguards*), 1960s. *Photograph by Cecil Layne. Courtesy of Terry Layne.*

The day of Bryant's funeral, the procession, led by Honi Coles, moved on past the Baby Grand, where Willie had hosted his radio show. It made its way past the Apollo Theater, where the Reuben Phillips Band, the house band, played Willie's theme song, "It's Over Because." Crowds had formed at the intersection of Seventh Avenue and 125th Street to wait for the procession. When the cortege arrived at the Hotel Theresa, the former home of Bryant, it stopped to bid good-bye to his favorite place and to acknowledge his loyal fans gathered there.

The year that Bryant died, Malcolm X had fallen out of favor with Elijah Muhammad, the head of the Nation of Islam. Newspaper accounts reported that Elijah Muhammad suspended Malcolm X for making negative and impudent remarks regarding the assassination of President John F. Kennedy during the national mourning period. Malcolm X promised to return to his position within the Nation of Islam by March of 1964 whether or not his suspension was lifted.

Malcolm X had befriended a young boxer named Cassius Clay, whom he met in the Hotel Theresa during this time. While Clay was living in the hotel during the spring of 1964, Malcolm took him under his wing, functioning as his "friend and religious adviser." The two visited African diplomats at the United Nations, and Malcolm escorted him to events around the New York area.

During the time that Ali and Malcolm X were spending time together, the singer Sam Cooke arrived at the Hotel Theresa. The three men hit it off and became friends. Sam Cooke had begun to take an interest in the Nation of Islam. Stories circulated around the Theresa that Malcolm X was recruiting Sam Cooke for the Nation of

Islam, and when Cooke was shot to death in a Los Angeles motel in 1964, literature from the Nation of Islam was in his room.

In March of 1964, Malcolm X and his family had traveled to Miami for the Cassius Clay–Sonny Liston fight. Harlem fight fans were overjoyed when Clay won. Harlem hadn't undergone such a jovial celebration since the days when Joe Louis held court at the Theresa. "I am the greatest," Clay said as he was crowned the heavyweight champion of the world. Harlem had seen him perform in the ring at a jam-packed Lowe's Victoria Theater down the street from the Theresa. They had spent $7.50 for a tickets while those in Miami who were ringside paid as much as $250. After Clay's heavyweight championship victory, the crowd shifted back to the Theresa's gold lounge, where they celebrated as hit tunes such as Martha and the Vandella's "Heat Wave," Jerry Butler's "Moon River" and "Precious Love," and the Impression's "It's All Right" blared from the jukebox.

The following morning, Clay stunned the world by announcing that his name was no longer Cassius Clay. He had been given the name Muhammad Ali by Elijah Muhammad. The twenty-two-year-old champion was a Black Muslim. There was buzz around the streets of Harlem that three African-American preachers from Ali's hometown in Louisville, Kentucky, had denounced Ali's newfound religious beliefs as an insult to his people and to America. These ministers were steeped in the philosophy of integration. What mattered most to them was that the Muslims believed in separatism. The ministers chastised Ali for taking money from a group of white men in Louisville who backed him.

Malcolm X said of Ali, "He will mean more to his people than

Muhammad Ali with fans, 1960s. *Photograph by John W. Mosley. Courtesy of the Charles L. Blockson Afro-American Collection, Temple University.*

any athlete before him. His is more than Jackie Robinson was, because Robinson is the white man's hero. But [Muhammad Ali] is the black man's hero . . . because the white man wants him to lose his heavyweight championship because he is black."

Ali had garnered a huge Harlem following just as Joe Louis had. He was now the most important black man in Harlem. That he made the Hotel Theresa his residence while in the city elevated the status of the once famous hotel to a small degree.

In an October 1964 *Playboy* interview, Ali talked about why it was important for him to make the Hotel Theresa, where he rented a three-room suite, his residence while in New York: "I could be living all exclusive, downtown, in some skyscraper hotel. I could be living right up in the hotel's penthouse. . . . I am up here in the heart of blacktown . . . but it seems to bother everybody else, it looks like. I been around my own people all of my life. Our people are warm people. I don't like being around cold people . . . You take Sonny Liston. He was the champion of the world, and that's supposed to include America. But when he tried to buy a house in a segregated neighborhood in Miami, he was turned down. The white people don't want integration: I don't believe in forcing it and the Muslims don't either."

Ali was experiencing a number of unwelcome visitors at the Theresa. He complained of women, both black and white, coming to his suite after midnight. They sent him their photographs, flowers, sweet-smelling notes with their phone numbers pleading with him to call them. Girls were bold enough to show up at his door masquerading as Muslims. Ali said no Muslim sister would ever have behaved in that manner.

Shortly after Ali's victory in Miami, there was a raid on Seventh Avenue and 125th Street. Word spread like lightning that six numbers runners were thrown into the wagon along with boxes of play slips. The federal agents confiscated some cash and a car in the raid. It was rumored that they had been watching people going in and out of the hotel and had taken movies of the action outside the area for a number of days.

"Sometimes, even if you hit the numbers, some of those cats wouldn't pay," said Danny Moore. "I hit once and went to collect from Sugar Ray's bar. The cat was so big and bad that I didn't even try to get my money. I even went and got Jackie Wilson's sidekick. He was a big guy. We went back and he saw the guy and he was scared to ask for the money."

Muhammad Ali is behind the podium. Louis Farrakhan is seated right, 1964.
Photograph by Cecil Layne. Courtesy of Terry Layne.

Theresa regular Red Dillion was arrested during this time. A federal grand jury had handed up a second indictment accusing the notorious underworld figure of conspiracy in the sale of narcotics. Dillion was sentenced to a ten-year prison term.

In the meantime, the rift between Malcolm X and Elijah Muhammad had grown wider. "It wasn't really the Kennedy statement," said businessman Percy Sutton. "It was Elijah Muhammad's having children with women other than his wife that Malcolm couldn't accept."

According to an *Amsterdam News* article, Elijah Muhammad had informed Malcolm X that he wouldn't be permitted to attend the Nation of Islam's annual convention in Chicago, which was held in late February of 1964. Malcolm X's suspension from the Muslim group was still in effect. Malcolm had grown even more powerful than Elijah Muhammad, his mentor and spiritual leader. In short, he had outgrown the Nation of Islam.

The rift existed not only between Elijah Muhammad and Malcolm X. Ali had chosen sides. He was in the Elijah Muhammad camp. "During my interviews with Clay in his three-room suite at Harlem's Theresa Hotel, inevitably the questions got around to Clay's Muslim membership, then to a query about what had happened to his formerly very close relationship with Malcolm X," said Alex Haley. "Evenly, Clay said, 'You don't buck Mr. Muhammad and get away with it. I don't want to talk about him no more.'"

Often thousands of people crowded into the intersection of Seventh Avenue and 125th Street to hear the teachings of the charismatic Malcolm X, who clearly understood the power of Harlem. Malcolm made it known that he would rather be an assistant minister in Harlem than a minister anywhere else in the country. James Booker noted that during the fifties Malcolm's main corner was 116th Street and Lenox Avenue. But as he became better known, he moved a bit farther uptown to the famous intersection. Malcolm X's rallies brought out enthusiastic crowds, including college students, hip cats, street activists, church leaders, and families, who all jammed into the intersection to hear him.

The famous intersection was called "the University of the Streets" because children and adults could get an education there. "And it was the beginning of why I call Malcolm X a master teacher. More than anything else, that's what he was," said the writer Peter Bailey. "Malcolm was a master teacher. He taught about the dangers of psychological oppression. Brother Malcolm attacked our minds. No other leader was talking about that. He never got riled up about Bull Connor or Governor Wallace. He never thought if we got rid of them, things would be cool."

"Malcolm was bold," said Percy Sutton. "He came along at a time when he was needed. The NAACP was picketing stores and obliged to take the route of God and country. Malcolm was not so obliged. He made the white man a scourge. A person standing at the gate to freedom. He created friction in American democracy. And that was healthy."

Gordon Parks recalled a foreboding incident. "I saw Malcolm for the very first time in person on the corner of Seventh Avenue and 125th Street, telling about four hundred white cops with guns on their hips what he thought about them. I thought, 'How long is this young man gonna live like this.' "

As the rift between Malcolm X and Elijah Muhammad grew

deeper, Malcolm X pondered establishing his own organization. "I am going to organize and head a new mosque in New York City known as the Organization of Afro-American Unity [OAAU] and Muslim Mosque Inc.," Malcolm X said to a reporter. "This will give us a religious base, and the spiritual force necessary to rid our people of the vices that destroy the moral fiber of our community. OAAU and Muslim Mosque will have its headquarters in the Hotel Theresa in Harlem. It will be the working base for an action program designed to eliminate the political oppression, the economic exploitation, and the social degradation suffered daily by twenty-two million Afro-Americans."

Love B. Woods rented Malcolm X the Carver Room in the Hotel Theresa for a meeting to discuss establishing an organization. Gossip throughout Harlem and among the Nation of Islam was that Malcolm X was intent on establishing a mosque in the Theresa. Malcolm X's offices were on the second floor of the hotel. The new organization didn't accept white membership. "How can there ever be white-black solidarity without black solidarity first?" Malcolm asserted. He did suggest that whites who were well meaning go into their own communities and educate others about the evils of racism.

When Malcolm returned from Mecca, he held a press conference in the Skyline Ballroom of the Theresa Hotel on May 21, 1964. "There must have been fifty still and television photographers and reporters jockeying for position, up front, and the rest of the Skyline Ballroom was filling with Negro followers of Malcolm X, or his well-wishers, and the curious," said the writer Alex Haley. Malcolm said, "I no longer subscribe to racism. I have adjusted my thinking to the point where I believe that whites are human beings as long as this is borne out by their humane attitude toward Negroes."

Malcolm X's organization's agenda was committed to the black man's right to self-defense, to determine his own destiny, and to fostering justice and equality.

"It was about a month before he was to go South that I walked into the Theresa Hotel to see him [Malcolm]," said the writer Ora Mobley. "He was alone. My stay with him was brief. I asked him, 'How are you?' He instantly replied, 'I understand I am going to be assassinated.' I was not shocked by his statement. About a year and a half before that, I had received a telephone call in which I was told that there was a plan to assassinate Malcolm. When I left the Hotel Theresa that day, it was with great pain in my heart. I knew so well how much he loved black people."

"Everybody disappeared from around the Theresa," recalled Delilah Jackson. "It was like a ghost town. The word was out that Malcolm X was going to be assassinated. Nobody went near the Theresa for nearly two weeks before his death."

The evening after Malcolm X was shot at the Audubon Ballroom, a crowd formed at the Hotel Theresa to wait for word on his condition. It was the most natural place for them to wait. While the phones were ringing in Malcolm's second-floor OAAU offices, the crowd outside the hotel grew. When they learned by transistor radio that Malcolm X was dead, they quietly cleared the intersection.

After Malcolm's death, Jimi Hendrix and Little Richard moved into the Theresa, on April 1, 1965. Jimi Hendrix played with various bands like King Curtis, Joey Dee and the Starlighters, and the Isley Brothers. Hendrix and Little Richard played in various clubs in

Greenwich Village during the next two years. In 1967, Hendrix left New York for London. Hendrix was probably the last celebrity to stay in the hotel before it became an office building and was renamed the Theresa Towers.

Love B. Woods had been in the hotel business since the 1920s. For most of his years as a hotelier, he dreamed of transforming the Hotel Theresa into the uptown Waldorf Astoria. But his dream turned to ashes by 1965. Woods had poured all of his capital into the purchase of the hotel nearly ten years before. In his resolve to manage a luxurious hotel for his people, he lost it all—his luxurious office building on 125th Street and the hotel—the final indignity of the Hotel Theresa.

EPILOGUE

The Hotel Theresa made headlines in September 1966 with the news it was being transformed into an office building. In fact, by the time of the announcement, renovations were already under way. A number tenants remained in the building, including Jimi Hendrix. The ground floor and five upper floors were being used for the Haryou Act Anti-Poverty Program. Black Muslim groups were leasing office space also. The purpose of converting the three-hundred-room hotel into an office building was to create a business district in Harlem. By then, major corporations were vying for space in the building. The Diamond Jewelry Store and Lewis Micheaux's African Memorial National Bookstore across the street from the hotel were being torn down to make way for Governor Nelson Rockefeller's $20-million state office building.

As a hotel, the fifty-four-year-old Theresa was financially threadbare. The new owners paid $1.25 million for the building. News that the Theresa now had white owners was disturbing for Harlem lawyer Dunbar McLaurin. McLaurin, a businessman, had attempted to buy the hotel but was unable to raise sufficient funds. "Blacks have had difficulty coming together on business deals," said one Harlem businessman. "Black entertainers have so many white

people controlling their money and business affairs. These account-
ants and lawyers tell them what to do. They sometimes stand between them and their own community. They aren't going to tell them
they should invest in Harlem. It's hard to get to black celebrities because they've got all these people surrounding them."

Segregation had given rise to the Theresa as the black world's
headquarters in an era when Jim Crow laws made blacks unwelcome
downtown—and in many places, uptown as well before the mid-
1940s. As a result, blacks gathered in the Theresa. Ironically, rising
antisegregation laws fueled the hotel's demise. A number of influential blacks who had played a role in Harlem's prominence and glamour had died or moved away by the time the hotel began to collapse.
The civil rights acts of the 1960s granted blacks freedom to purchase houses in white neighborhoods and a wider selection of downtown hotels to patronize. These new civil rights laws enabled certain
blacks to become homeowners in suburban areas like Long Island,
Westchester County, and various northern New Jersey townships.
Those outside the community found no reason to visit Harlem anymore. The novelty of "slumming uptown" wore off. "The heyday of
Negro entertainment is long gone," a Harlem newspaper columnist
wrote. "Nobody comes to Harlem anymore. Nobody seems to care.
. . . Only a few places offer anything approaching a show, and even
so it's nothing like the days when 'Harlem jumped.' " No prominent
person would consider checking into the Theresa. The Harlem that
Duke Ellington had once described as the "scenes from the *Arabian
Nights*" was gone, and the Hotel Theresa went with it.

Years before the hotel closed, a number of its former year-round
residents and a few regulars had moved to Harlem's new highrise de-

velopment, the Lenox Terrace Complex. They were Jackie "Moms" Mabley, Grace Nail Johnson, Bill Brown, Ron Brown, Jewel Sims Okala, Ruth Brown, Anna Arnold Hedgeman, and Percy Sutton. Gloria Brown, now divorced from Bill, had returned to Washington, D.C. But a number of movers and shakers had abandoned Harlem. Billy Rowe sold his Harlem brownstone and bought a house in Westchester County. Thurgood Marshall traded in Sugar Hill for Washington, D.C., when he was appointed as Solicitor General and in 1966 to the U.S. Supreme Court. Celebrities like Sugar Ray Robinson, Nat King Cole, Joe Louis, Billy Eckstine, Sidney Poitier, and Lena Horne were living on the West Coast.

In 1967, Congressman Adam Clayton Powell Jr. was stripped of his committee chairmanship based on a pending investigation by the Judiciary Committee. By 1970, he was no longer representing Harlem in Congress. He was replaced by Charles Rangel, who had served as the desk clerk at the Theresa Hotel while he attended law school.

No one is certain what kind of neighborhood Harlem will be in the twenty-first century. The neighborhood is undergoing major changes once again. A gentrification movement is well under way, and a new luxury hotel is going up just two blocks east of the old Hotel Theresa. As Percy Sutton has said, "Everybody's coming to Harlem." Something is always lost and gained with change. Social change often moves with a deliberate rhythm, and a "Hotel Theresa heyday" will definitely come again for a new generation.

The question on the minds of Harlemites today was asked by James Weldon Johnson seventy-five years ago. Are blacks going to be able to hold Harlem, a black city located in the heart of white Manhattan, arguably the most expensive island in the world? Johnson argued all those years ago, "When colored people do leave Harlem, their homes, their churches, their investments, and their businesses, it will be because the land has become so valuable they can no longer afford to live on it."

WHERE HAVE THEY GONE?

The story of the Hotel Theresa involved countless people. For nearly thirty years of the twentieth century, the broadest diversity of African-Americans stayed under one roof. The majority of the stories in this book are based on interviews and firsthand accounts. Write a biography of a person, and there will always be those who could tell more and don't; but write a biography of a hotel, indeed of an era, and everyone has something to say. There's a cachet to having been there. The contributors to this book brought a wealth of information on the social, political, economic, and cultural history of Harlem—stories that have never been in print. It is their hope that this story about one of the major social and cultural institutions that was lost in Harlem's decline will enable the reader to gain a deeper understanding of the personalities of the men and women who were at the center of black thought and action for almost three decades. A number of the contributors were enduring life-threatening health problems. Nevertheless, they were eager to participate because they understood that they had witnessed history in the making. The following, although not a comprehensive list, reveals what happened to them after the demise of the Hotel Theresa.

Muhammad Ali (Cassius Clay), currently one of the most beloved figures in the world, the three time world heavyweight boxing champion of the world, serves as United Nations Messenger of Peace. He suffers from Parkinson's disease. The sixty-one-year-old ex-champion and his fourth wife, Lonnie Ali, are active with the Michael J. Fox Foundation for Parkinson's disease. Today, Lonnie Ali manages and coordinates Muhammad Ali's charities. The Ali family lives on a farm in Michigan.

Lee Archer was a Tuskegee Airman and is a retired businessman who lives in Westchester County, New York.

Peter Bailey was working for the Organization of Afro-American Unity (OAAU) in the Hotel Theresa at the time of Malcolm X's death in 1965. He lives in Washington, D.C., where he contributes articles to a number of publications.

Charles L. Blockson is curator for the Charles L. Blockson Afro-American Collection, at Temple University. One of the foremost bibliophiles in the nation, he is the author of several books on African-American history, including the *Underground Railroad.* He lives in suburban Pennsylvania.

James Booker Sr. still writes for various New York papers. He serves on a number of municipal organizations. He and his wife, the former Jean Williams, live in Harlem, New York.

Herb Boyd lives in Harlem, where he writes for the *New York Amsterdam News.* He teaches at the College of New Rochelle. He is currently writing a biography of Sugar Ray Robinson.

William (Bill) Harmon Brown left the Theresa in 1959. After moving to Lenox Terrace, he tried a number of jobs: bail bondsman and hair products supply salesman. He continued his gambling parties in Lenox Terrace. Bill Brown traveled to the Democratic presidential convention in Atlanta in 1988 at the invitation of his son. He died that same year of heart failure.

John Henrik Clarke was a world-renowned historian. For a number of years he taught African-American studies at Hunter College, where he mentored countless students. He died in New York City in 1998.

Frances (Miller) Cohen, an antique collector, lived on East 57th Street in New York. Mrs. Cohen died in 1952 in New York City.

Naidine Collins lives in New York City, where she enjoys the company of her two French poodles.

Marjorie Corbitt was born and raised in Harlem. She worked for a state agency until her retirement in the 1970s. Marjorie Corbitt died in 2000.

Evelyn Cunningham was a columnist for the New York office of the *Pittsburgh Courier* during the Hotel Theresa's heyday. She currently contributes articles to a number of publications. She lives in New York City.

Mattye Jean Davis-Foreman was a graduate of Howard University. She served as switchboard operator for the Hotel Theresa during the 1940s and 1950s. While working at the hotel, Mattye Jean was in a number of Broadway musicals. She taught school for the New York City Board of Education until her retirement in the 1991. She died in 1993.

Ophelia DeVore was one of the first black models during the 1940s. She is founder and president of Grace Del Marco Modeling Agency. Miss DeVore enjoys spending time with her five children and grandchildren. She lives in New York City.

Hazel Ferebee served as office manager and bookkeeper for the dental practice of her husband (Dr. T. Claude Ferebee) in New York City until their retirement in 1989. She lives in Selma, Alabama.

David Goldman is the current manager of the Theresa Towers. His office is located in Brooklyn, New York.

Ruth Guzzman is a retired barmaid (mixoclologist). She lives in New York City where she enjoys spending time with her family.

Susie H. operated a catering and bootleg liquor business from her home in Toledo, Ohio. She had a special interest in homeless persons. She died in 2003.

Anna Arnold Hedgeman moved from the Hotel Theresa to the Lenox Terrace Apartments in 1958 with her husband, the classical singer Merritt Hedgeman. She was the first black female in the cabinet of Mayor Robert Wagner. She was outspoken on civil rights and women's issues until her death in 1988.

Chuck Jackson became a household name when his song "Any Day Now" hit the top of the charts in the 1960s. He continues to tour with his music. He lives in New York City with his wife, Helen.

Hal Jackson is one of the most popular personalities in radio and television history. Having been on the radio since the 1930s, he is group chairman of Inner City Broadcasting Company and executive producer and host of Talented Teens International Competition. He lives in New York City with his wife, Debi.

KennerBelle Jackson was a vaudeville actress. She was an avid reader and enjoyed crossword puzzles and traveling. She died in 1997.

Illinois Jacquet's hit song "Flying Home" made him one of the most famous musicians in the nation during the 1940s. Jacquet continues to work as a musician. He lives in Queens, New York.

Grace Nail Johnson moved into the Lenox Terrace Apartments after leaving the Hotel Theresa. She spent the remainder of her life perpetuating the legacy of her husband, the writer and civil rights leader James Weldon Johnson. She died at her home in Harlem on November 1, 1976, at the age of ninety-one.

Ludie Jones dances with the famous Harlem Seniors' Dancing Silver Belles. She lives in New York City.

Nick Jones has retired from the pharmaceutical business. He lives in New York City.

Charles Kenyatta was a bodyguard for Malcolm X and was a Harlem orator. Currently, he is a Baptist minister in New York City.

Terry Layne was a concert singer. She worked as an assistant to her husband, the photographer Cecil Layne. She enjoys playing bridge and participating in charitable work. Mrs. Layne lives in New York City.

Debbie McDade was a waitress in the coffee shop of the Hotel Theresa. She wrote songs and performed while working at the Theresa. Mrs. McDade currently lives in Fort Lauderdale, Florida. She enjoys visiting New York to see old friends.

Leroy Meyers was a professional dancer. Today he mentors young dancers and can be found at Showman's, a popular Harlem nightspot.

Trumpeter Danny Moore continues to perform as a museum piece with the Danny Moore Quintet for parties, weddings, and social events in the Northeast.

John Nailor is one of the foremost orthopedic surgeons in the nation. He was a lifelong friend of the late Ron Brown's. He lives in New York City.

Fayard Nicholas was the part of the famous dancing duo the Nicholas brothers. He lives in Los Angeles, California, with his wife, Katherine.

[Ollie] **Jewel Sims Okala** was the first African-American supervisor of nursing at New York's Roosevelt Hospital. After she retired from nursing in 1970, she did volunteer work for the elderly. She died in 2001.

Adam Clayton Powell Jr. served in Congress from 1945 to 1971. During his tenure in Congress, he served as chairman on the Committee on Education and Labor. In 1967 he was excluded from being sworn in based on on a pending investigation by the House Judiciary Committee. He was reelected November 5, 1968, and served until January 3, 1971. His unsuccessful bid for the Democratic nomination made Charles B. Rangel the victor. Powell died of cancer in Miami, Florida, on April 4, 1972.

Charles B. Rangel was elected to Congress in 1970 to succeed Adam Clayton Powell Jr. As one of the most effective legislators, he is the ranking member on the Ways and Means Committee. He lives in Harlem, New York.

Edna Mae Robinson lived in New York City until her death in 2002. During the last years of her life, she taught dancing and exercise classes to the elderly.

Billy Rowe was born in Columbia, South Carolina, and moved to New York as a young boy. He began submitting columns to the *Pittsburgh Courier* in the mid-1930s. In 1940, he started writing the popular weekly column "Billy Rowe's Notebook." During World War I and for years afterward, the *Courier* was the most influential black newspaper in the nation. Rowe's popular column had a lot to do with the *Courier*'s success. In 1953, he was named a New York City deputy police commissioner. A few years later, he joined Joe Louis and founded the public relations firm of Louis and Rowe. He died in 1997 in Westchester County, New York.

Betty Stanton lives in Harlem. She rarely leaves her home.

Percy Sutton is chairman emeritus of InnerCity Broadcasting Company. He remains active in the business and civil rights communities. He lives in Harlem, New York.

Judge James Watson was appointed to the U.S. Customs Court by President Lyndon B. Johnson in 1966, and served with distinction until his death in 2001. A veteran of World War II, Judge Watson earned the Purple Heart, the Battle Star, and the Combat Infantry Badge.

Preston Wilcox works as a researcher, teacher, and archivist. He spends much of his time mentoring students and writers on the history of Harlem. He lives in New York City.

Joe Wilder is a native of Philadelphia. He played with some of the greatest orchestra leaders, including Jimmie Lunceford, Lucky Millinder, Duke Ellington, and Cab Calloway. He remains active as a musician. He lives in New York City.

Bibliography

The literature on the Hotel Theresa is minuscule; therefore, *Meet Me at the Theresa: The Story of Harlem's Most Famous Hotel* is primarily based on interviews. A number of columnists wrote stories on the hotel based on firsthand experiences. These articles were useful in developing the story.

In my effort to reconstruct the history of Harlem, numerous works offered a clear path. Harlem's history can only be explained by an understanding of how African-Americans became inhabitants of the Manhattan Island. Primary source material on the subject can be found in research papers prepared by the WPA Writers' Program. These papers shed light upon aspects of African-American life in Manhattan when whites inhabited Harlem and blacks lived in lower Manhattan. This book also touches on the black experience in New York during the early twentieth century, and finally, the birth of black Harlem. Other pioneering works on Harlem that were useful include James Weldon Johnson's *Black Manhattan* and Jervis Anderson's *This Was Harlem: 1900–1950*.

Books

Anderson, Jervis. *This Was Harlem: 1900–1950*. New York: Farrar, Straus & Giroux, 1981.

Baker, Jean Claude, and Chris Chase. *Josephine: The Josephine Baker Story*. New York: Random House, 1993.

Birmingham, Stephen. *Certain People: America's Black Elite.* Boston: Little, Brown and Company, 1977.

Blumenthal, Ralph. *The Stork Club: America's Most Famous Nightspot and the Lost World of Café Society.* Boston: Little, Brown and Company, 2000.

Boyd, Herb, ed. *The Harlem Reader: A Celebration of New York's Most Famous Neighborhood, From the Renaissance Years to the 21st Century.* New York: Three Rivers Press, 2003.

———. *"Sugar in Harlem: The Biography of Sugar Ray Robinson."* Unpublished manuscript.

Brown, Tracey L. *The Life and Times of Ron Brown: A Memoir by His Daughter.* New York: William Morrow and Company, 1998.

Feather, Leonard. *The Encyclopedia of Jazz.* New York: Horizon Press, 1960.

Gribin, Anthony J., and Matthew M. Schiff. *The Complete Book of Doo-Wop.* Iola, WI: Krause Publications, 2000.

Groia, Philip. *They All Sang on the Corner.* Port Jefferson, NY: Phillie Dee Enterprises, 1983.

History of Blacks in Film. Los Angeles: The William Grant Still Community Arts Center, 1983.

Holmes, Stephen. *Ron Brown: An Uncommon Life.* New York: John Wiley Sons, Inc., 2000.

Huggins, Nathan Irvin. *Harlem Renaissance.* New York: Oxford University Press, 1971.

Jackson, Hal. *The House That Jack Built: My Life as a Trailblazer in Broadcasting and Entertainment.* New York: Amistad Press, 2001.

Johnson, James Weldon. *Black Manhattan.* New York: Alfred A. Knopf, 1930.

Lawrenson, Helen. *Stranger at the Party: A Memoir.* New York: Random House, 1972.

Lewis, David Levering. *When Harlem Was in Vogue.* New York: Oxford University Press, 1982.

Louis, Joe, with Edna and Art Rust Jr. *Joe Louis: My Life*. New York: Harcourt Brace Jovanovich, 1978.

Malcolm X, with Alex Haley. *The Autobiography of Malcolm X*. New York: Grove Press, 1965.

Osofsky, Gilbert. *Harlem: The Making of a Ghetto*. New York: HarperCollins, 1971.

Schiffman, Jack. *Harlem's Heyday*. Buffalo, NY: Prometheus, 1979.

Smith, Marvin. *Harlem: The Vision of Morgan and Marvin Smith*. Lexington: University of Kentucky Press, 1998.

Sweeting, Ora Mobley, and Ezekiel C. Mobley Jr. *Nobody Gave Me Permission*. Xlibris Corporation, 2000.

Wilkins, Roy. *Standing Fast: The Autobiography of Roy Wilkins*. New York: Viking Press, 1982.

Wilson, Sondra Kathryn, ed. *The Crisis Reader: Stories, Poems, and Essays from the Crisis Magazine*. New York: Random House, 1999.

Newspapers and Periodicals

The Age (New York), 1940–67

Amsterdam News (New York), 1940–67

Ebony, April 1946–65

Harper's, April 1948

Jet, 1957–64

Negro Digest, 1944–50

The New York Times, 1941, 1967

The Pittsburgh Courier, 1940–67

Personal Interviews

Lee Archer, New Rochelle, New York, 20 August 2003

Peter Bailey, Washington, DC, 22 August 2003

Jean Claude Baker, New York City, 10 November 2003

Yvonne Benjamin, New York City, 24 October 2003

Charles L. Blockson, Philadelphia, PA, 23 September 2003

James Booker Sr., New York City, 8 and 11 August 2000

Jean Williams Booker, New York City, 4 October 2003

Herb Boyd, New York City, 24 November 2002

Jim Carter, New York City, 12 June 2002

John Henrik Clarke, New York City, 3 March 1997

Alfred Cobb, New York City, 2 April 2000

Naidine Collins, New York City, 14 January 2000, 11 October 2000

Marjorie Corbitt, New York City, 3 and 6 August 1999

Evelyn Cunningham, New York City, 2 and 5 August 2000, 12 and 24 February 2002

Ophelia DeVore, New York City, 12 June 2002

Joan Fairservis, New York City, 14 August 2001

Hazel Ferebee, Selma, AL, 14 August 2002

David Goldman, Brooklyn, NY, 2 August 2002

Jeff Greenup, New York City, 6 September 2003

Johnny Grimes, New York City, 4 August 2002

Rosa Guy, New York City, 12 May 2003

Ruth Guzzman, New York City, 2 and 6 August 2002

Susie Heard, Toledo, OH, 3 July 2002

Chuck Jackson, New York City, 1 August 2000

Delilah Jackson, New York City, 3 June 2000, 15 March 2001

KennerBelle Jackson, Toledo, OH, 2 January 1997

Illinois Jacquet, New York City, 12 February 2003

Vernon Jarrett, Chicago, IL, 3 March 2001

William Johnson, Detroit, MI, 7 June 2001

Ludie Jones, New York City, 8 September 2001, 17 November 2001

Nick Jones, New York City, 13 October 2002

Murray Kay, New York City, 11 October 2002

Charles Kenyatta, New York City, 2 August 2003

Terry Layne, New York City, 2 August 2000

Debbie McDade, Fort Lauderdale, FL, 23 September 2001

Jake McKnight, New York City, 21 October 2003

Leroy Meyers, New York City, 23 March 2001, 2 April 2001

Danny Moore, New York City, 2 September 2003, 12 and 14 October 2003

Rose Morgan, Chicago, IL, 2 June 2003

John Nailor, New York City, 23 July 2003

Fayard Nicholas, Los Angeles, CA, 2 April 2003

[Ollie] Jewel Sims Okala, New York City, 12 April 1997, 10 and 14 December 1998

Paula Owens, New York City, 12 August 2003

Mary Pitman, New York City, 3 February 2000

Charles Rangel, New York City, 19 July 2003

Priscilla Sims, Little Rock, AK, 8 August 2003

Betty Stanton, 2 May 2000, 12 and 13 June 2000

Percy Sutton, New York City, June 17, 2003

Bob Tate, New York City, 13 October 2002

Billy Vera, Los Angeles, CA, 3 February 2003

Judge James Watson, New York City, 30 July and 1 August 2000

Preston Wilcox, New York City, 12 and 14 June 2003

Frazelle Williams, New York City, 10 May 2003

Mary Louise Williams, New York City, 12 October 2002, 23 October 2003

Notes

THE NEIGHBORHOOD

5 This two-way artery: Jervis Anderson, *This Was Harlem: 1900–1950* (New York: Farrar, Straus & Giroux, 1981), 319.

5 "A grand thoroughfare": Ibid.

7 "If we couldn't find": Ibid., 320.

9 "The employment policy at Blumstein's": *Amsterdam News,* March 21, 1953.

9 In 1958, Martin Luther King Jr.: Hal Jackson, *The House That Jack Built* (New York: Amistad Press, 2001), 123.

9 "I used to walk": Jack Schiffman, *Harlem's Heyday* (Buffalo, NY: Prometheus, 1979), 72.

A PLACE TO UNITE

15 "Josephine had done": Jean Claude Baker and Chris Chase, *Josephine: The Josephine Baker Story* (New York: Random House, 1993), 306.

16 "When my husband called": Ibid.

17 "This is something which": *Amsterdam News,* November 23, 1951.

17 "Bessie could sell herself": Baker and Chase, *Josephine Baker Story,* 307.

17 "The American way of life": *Pittsburgh Courier,* June 15, 1941.

19 "Well, what I started": Joe Louis with Edna and Art Rust Jr., *My Life* (New York: Harcourt Brace Javonovich, 1978), 112.

20 "I remember visiting Billy": Schiffman, *Harlem Heyday,* 113.

21 "In the Theresa's heyday": Tony Scherman, "The Theresa," *The American Legacy,* Winter 1998.

THE SIDEWALK CAPTAINS

25 "We are, to put": *Amsterdam News,* October 30, 1953.

25 "It was a gold mine": Helen Lawrenson, *Stranger at the Party: A Memoir* (New York: Random House, 1972).

29 "Now, Billy was a": Louis *My Life,* 76.

THE QUEEN'S CORONATION

49 "There are no restaurants": Anderson, *This Was Harlem,* 28.

49 arduous metamorphosis as it went: James Weldon Johnson, *Black Manhattan* (New York: Alfred A. Knopf, 1930), 3.

54 "To get even, one": Anderson, *This Was Harlem,* 52.

55 "All around Seventh Avenue": *Ebony,* April 1946.

56 "the finest in entertainment": See Jervis Anderson's *This Was Harlem,* page 47, for description of Seventh Avenue around 1911 when the Hotel Theresa was being built.

59 "When I moved to": Scherman, "Theresa"; and interview with Alfred Cobbs.

59 "There were two places": Lawrenson, *Stranger at the Party,* 170.

59 "We ain't no zoo": Ibid., 171.

61–62 "Men walking along the": "Bubbling Brown Sugar," brochure circa 1970s.

66 "We've got the top": *Ebony,* April 1946.

67 "I like it here": Ibid.

CELEBRITIES AND NIGHTLIFE

77 "As far as I'm": Schiffman, *Harlem's Heyday,* 102.

78 "When a young kid": Jackson, *House That Jack Built,* 118.

81 Cuningham and Walker admitted: Louis, *My Life,* 134; and interview with Evelyn Cunningham. Joe Louis and Evelyn Cunningham both witnessed the heavy drinking of Tallulah Bankhead.

BACK DOOR STUFF (1940–48)

82–83 "There were so many": Stephen Holmes, *Ron Brown: An Uncommon Life,* (New York: John Wiley Sons, 2000), 20, and interviews with Evelyn Cunningham and Albert Murray.

85 "There were always crowds": Scherman, Theresa; and interview with Albert Murray.

87 In 1940, only 12: Holmes, *Ron Brown,* 23. *A New York Age* article dated March 20, 1940, discusses the census report and its impact on African-Americans.

94 Walter Scott proudly claimed: See *Ebony,* April 1946, for a description of the inside of the Hotel Theresa.

94 "The bar was a crossroads": Scherman, "Theresa." A number of interviewees referred to the Theresa's bar as a crossroads.

95 "If a guy gets": *Ebony,* April 1946.

95 "All the glasses from": Ibid.

99 "He was a Harlem legend": Lawrenson, *Stranger at the Party,* 163.

103 "We were standing at": Ibid., 164.

107 "Edna Mae was simply": Herb Boyd, "Sugar in Harlem: The Biography of Sugar Ray Robinson," unpublished manuscript). In virtually every conversation about Edna Mae, all who knew her agreed that she was beautiful.

108 "Ray's mother didn't want": Ibid.

108 "Edna Mae is fourth": Ibid.

110 mezzanine was comfortably filled: See *Ebony,* April 1946, for description of inside of the Hotel Theresa.

114 Suites with sitting rooms: Ibid.

119–120 Not everybody was happy: Ibid.

124 "Baron Smith's image and": Sidney Poitier, "Life in Black and White," in Herb Boyd, ed., *The Harlem Reader* (New York: Three Rivers Press, 2003), 159.

THE JOE LOUIS ERA

132 "Max and I were": Louis, *My Life,* 44.

132 "The people in Harlem": Ibid., 67.

136 "I knew I had": Ibid., 95.

BILL BROWN'S DEBUT (1948–58)

140–141 Information on the early life of Bill Brown can be found in Stephen Holmes's *Ron Brown: An Uncommon Life.*

142 "Gloria was always a lovable": Ibid., 14.

143 "Martha, you should buy": Ibid., 25.

147 "Bill had a lot": Ibid., 22.

147 "My grandfather loved that": Scherman, "Theresa."

147–148 "He [Ronnie] left Harlem: Holmes, *Ron Brown,* 21.

148 "My father's childhood friends": Tracey L. Brown, *The Life and Times of Ron Brown: A Memoir by His Daughter* (New York: William Morrow and Company, 1998), 44.

149 "What an active little": Holmes, *Ron Brown,* 22.

149 "Dad was intrepid": Brown, *Ron Brown,* 43.

149 "My earliest years were": Holmes, *Ron Brown,* 21.

150 "Dad spent a lot": Brown, *Ron Brown,* 49.

152 At night, from its: Holmes, *Ron Brown,* 22.

153 "If you had a wedding": Brown, *Ron Brown*, 41.

155 "Gloria was such a": Holmes, *Ron Brown*, 26.

157 "Everyone knew Bumpy, and": Lawrenson, *Stranger at the Party*, 56.

MIXING IT UP

176 "Everywhere he went he": Boyd, "Sugar in Harlem."

185 "There was a preponderance": Jackson, *House That Jack Built*, 116.

186 "I took advantage of": Ibid., 57.

187 "Berry Gordy and Marv": Ibid., 165.

187–189 "It was in the": Ibid., 155.

THE INTERNATIONAL SPOTLIGHT
ON THE HOTEL THERESA

211 "Wasn't no Communist country": Maya Angelou, "Castro in Cuba," in Boyd, *Harlem Reader*, 223.

215 "Mother, I guess you'll": Ibid., 224.

215–216 "I am delighted to": From speech by John F. Kennedy in front of the Hotel Theresa, October 12, 1960.

THE FINAL DAYS

229 for a meeting to discuss: Malcolm X and Alex Haley, *The Autobiography of Malcolm X* (New York: Grove Press) 320.

229 "How can there ever": Ibid., 402.

229 "There must have been fifty": Ibid., 414.

230 "It was about a": "African Independence, Black Consciousness," in Ora Mobley Sweeting and Ezekiel C. Mobley Jr., *Nobody Gave Me Permission* (X libris Corporation, 2000).

Index

Note: Page numbers in *italics* refer to illustrations.

ABOUT THE AUTHOR

Dr. Sondra Kathryn Wilson is an associate at the W. E. B. Du Bois Institute, Harvard University; founder and president of the James Weldon Johnson Foundation, Inc.; and executor of James Weldon Johnson's literary estate. Her publications include *Lift Every Voice and Sing: A Celebration of the Negro National Anthem, 100 Years, 100 Voices*, coedited with Julian Bond (winner of the NAACP Image Award for Outstanding Literary Work, 2001). As editor of Random House's Harlem Renaissance Series, she edited *The Crisis Reader, The Opportunity Reader,* and *The Messenger Reader.* Other books include *In Search of Democracy* and *James Weldon Johnson: Complete Poetry.* She is currently writing the history of the National Association for the Advancement of Colored People (NAACP). She lives in New York City.

Printed in the United States
By Bookmasters